THE GREAT BEAR RAINFOREST

HARBOUR PUBLISHING

THE **GREAT BEAR RAINFOREST**
Canada's Forgotten Coast

Ian McAllister & Karen McAllister
with Cameron Young

Photography by Ian McAllister

Foreword by Robert F. Kennedy Jr.

5th printing, 2007

Published by Harbour Publishing
P.O. Box 219
Madeira Park, BC
V0N 2H0 Canada
www.harbourpublishing.com

Page design and composition by Frances Hunter.
Art direction by Roger Handling, Terra Firma Digital Arts.
Illustrations by Kim LaFave. Cartography by Baden Cross, Tim
Wilson.

Photograph of dolphin on page 37 by Brian Falconer,
photograph of Namu Dig on page 63 by Peter McAllister,
photograph of salmon on page 74 by Bernadette Mertens,
photograph of Larry Jorgenson on page 80 by Doug Cowell.
All other photographs by Ian McAllister.

The images of wildlife in this book are all of wild animals
in their natural habitat. Nikon 35mm equipment was used,
and occasionally a Pentax 67 for medium-format work. Fuji
Velvia film was used almost exclusively, with some Provia and
Kodachrome 200.

Canadian Cataloguing in Publication Data

McAllister, Ian, 1969-
    The great bear rainforest

ISBN 1-55017-166-6 / 978-1-55017-166-2

    1. Pacific Coast (B.C.)—Pictorial works. 2. Forest
conservation—British Columbia—Pacific Coast.
3. Forest ecology—British Columbia—Pacific Coast.
I. McAllister, Karen, 1969- II. Young, Cameron, 1944-
III. Title.
FC3845.P2M32 1997   917.11'1044'0222
C97-910749-0   F1089.P2M32 1997

Printed in China on acid-free, chlorine-free paper containing
post-consumer waste fibre.

CONTENTS

British Columbia is home to the planet's last large expanse of coastal temperate rainforest. The forest carpets a topography of stunning geological relief, and its forest's rugged beauty, tremendous biological diversity and vast unspoiled range set it apart as one of nature's great masterpieces. The temperate coniferous rainforest is one of the earth's most diverse ecosystems, providing habitat for endangered and threatened species including salmon, wolves, eagles, and grizzly and Kermode bears. Its biological productivity is unmatched, with a biomass of 500 tons per acre, 40 percent greater than tropical forests. On my first visits to the forests of the BC coast in the early 1990s, I found a setting that exceeded all my expectations, a place where snow-capped mountains crowd the estuaries they feed with fresh water and nutrients. I hiked on snowshoes across the wide mudflats that form the second finest migratory staging ground in western Canada, providing vital sustenance for seventy-eight waterfowl species. I gathered oysters and caught coho salmon and cooked them on the shore, and I followed wolf tracks through narrow mountain gorges beneath hemlock, giant cedar, Sitka spruce and thundering waterfalls. I saw great rookeries of sea lions and bald eagles congregate for the herring run and watched fishermen harvest geoduck clams. If we ever had country like that in the United States, we've long since destroyed it with failed forestry practices.

In addition to its aesthetic and biological features, the rainforest is the centrepiece for British Columbia's tourist and fishing industries which will play important roles in the sustainable vitality of the area's economy. The forest is also home to First Nations peoples whose spiritual and cultural life is tied to its health. Unfortunately, irresponsible development and the lack of protection for the forest have left these unique cultures and the entire ecosystem in grave danger.

The British Columbia government has recently begun to recognize the importance of its north coast rainforest by setting aside small tracts as parks. These fragments are far too limited to sustain forest diversity. For example, grizzly bears, for which the northern BC raincoast is prime habitat, often travel many miles in one day. The species will not survive in a scattered patchwork of small parks. As forest ecologist Jerry Franklin says, "the fragmentation turns plants and animals into virtual island dwellers, often with no acceptable way to travel from one remnant of habitat to another."

Ecologists are reporting the ominous deterioration associated with "Island Ecology" in systems as diverse as Yellowstone, Banff and the Serengeti. These same ecologists are now questioning whether any of the world's great parks is large enough to avoid steady ecosystem decline. As we enter the millennium, will every last elephant and grizzly bear be dependent on some degree of artificial life support?

These sobering questions are precisely why British Columbia's northern mainland coast deserves to be at the top of every conservation agenda. This forest region possesses the rarest of all environmental qualities: critical mass. At 8 million acres (3.2 million hectares) the whole Great Bear Rainforest is 9 times the size of the Olympic National Park, 5 times the size of Banff National Park and twice the size of the Serengeti—although the actual extent of productive forest amid all this wild landscape is a more modest 560,000 acres (224,000 hectares). It presents humankind with an opportunity, one which has already been lost elsewhere—to protect enough of one major ecosystem to guarantee the survival of all its components. Canada has the chance to create a world class natural attraction, store biodiversity and hedge against global climate change.

We know from experience in Oregon and Washington that the big logging companies will cut timber to the point of economic collapse. The BC provincial government's decision to encourage the hasty liquidation of these forests for cash through the most destructive practices of industrial logging is a global tragedy.

I hope this book will help awaken people to the importance of this last magnificent stand of the great North American rainforest. If it is destroyed, history will not judge us harshly because few will know the magnificence that has been lost. Those of us who remember will only be able to open this book and say to our children, in Norman Maclean's lament, "Oh what a wonderful world it was." ■

The landscape of British Columbia's northern coast presents a breathtaking panorama. Gribbell Island is shown here, with Ursula Channel at left and Verney Passage at right.

The province of British Columbia on Canada's Pacific coast has long been renowned for the beauty of its coastal landscape and the rich complexity of its temperate rainforest, a rare ecosystem that at its peak covered only one-fifth of 1 percent of the earth's land mass. In recent decades BC has unfortunately gained another reputation—for degrading these great natural treasures by clearcut logging, overfishing and other forms of development. Names like Carmanah Valley and Clayoquot Sound became household words as activists around the world rallied to save a few enclaves of southern BC's magnificent old-growth trees from the clearcutter's blade.

What has been overlooked in the struggle to save these remnant unlogged watersheds on the southern half of British Columbia's coast is that the province has a spectacular northern coast which is also blessed with temperate rainforests of great age and immense biological richness. The difference is that the northern raincoast has survived into the twenty-first century with comparatively little disturbance and its ancient rainforest ecology remains largely intact.

From the top end of Vancouver Island for 400 kilometres north along the Inside Passage to the Alaska border, a coastal wilderness the size of two Switzerlands sprawls among a maze of islands and inlets that, if it were untangled in a straight line, would stretch 16,000 kilometres. This largely unoccupied and unknown coastal labyrinth shelters a hidden universe of pristine river valleys and fiords dense with wildfowl, bald eagles, salmon, sea lions, porpoise, whales, timber wolves, black bears, Canada's largest grizzly bears, and the rare all-white spirit bear or Kermode bear. Every kilometre teems with gemlike islands, crystalline lakes and streams and majestic waterfalls, hundreds of them still unnamed. It is one of the last places on earth where you can spend weeks sailing or hiking in enchanting rainforest surroundings without seeing any sign of human society, although the area is home to the most isolated and independent First Nations tribes left in coastal North America. The northern BC raincoast is unquestionably the most unspoiled temperate rainforest left on the planet, and unlike almost every other rainforest preserve, it is large enough to be self-sustaining on an indefinite basis.

For those who have despaired of the earth's vanishing rainforest being saved, the news seems almost too good to be true, but it comes with an ominous proviso. Having cut through the more accessible and merchantable forests of the southern coast, British Columbia's voracious timber industry has turned its attention to the virgin forest of the north coast and has already ravaged some of the most productive watersheds. Virtually every one of the eighty-odd major undisturbed drainages in the northern region is under application for clearcutting by large forest companies, and if no decisive action is taken in the next several years, the opportunity to save the planet's most important rainforest wilderness will be lost.

Ian and Karen McAllister, two Canadian conservationists whose studies first led them to the northern BC coast in 1990, immediately became alarmed at the fate about to befall this magnificent rainforest holdout. For the next seven years they dedicated every day and every dollar they could muster to exploring the region and documenting its magnificence on film and in words so they could make the world aware of what was at stake. Their effort, which at one point involved circling most of North America in a small trimaran which was their home base, has been prodigious. This book reflects both the grandeur of their cause and the passion of their commitment. ■

The Ecstall River near Prince Rupert runs through the largest unprotected intact rainforest valley on the northern BC coast.

INTRODUCTION
by IAN McALLISTER

Who would have guessed that a single river valley would change our lives completely? It was spring 1990 when we first heard the rumour about a spectacular river valley hidden up on the north coast of British Columbia. This place was said to be full of grizzly bears that walked white sandy beaches and lived in the lush rainforest surrounding the Koeye—a magnificent river full of salmon. We could not even pronounce the word Koeye ("K'way"), much less imagine what it looked like. All we knew was that it was beautiful, MacMillan Bloedel had plans to log it, and a developer was going to build a big resort at the mouth. It was time to visit the Koeye.

A grizzly bear searches the Koeye River estuary for carcasses of spawned-out salmon.

USA

ALASKA

Masset

Prince
Rupert

Kitimat

HAIDA GWAII

QUEEN CHARLOTTE ISLANDS

Hartley
Bay

PRINCESS
ROYAL
ISLAND

Hecate Strait

Klemtu

Bella
Coola

Bella Bella

Koeye
River

Queen
Charlotte
Sound

Rivers
Inlet

Cape Caution

Knight
Inlet

Bute
Inlet

Cape Scott

Port
Hardy

Pacific
Ocean

BRITISH

COLUMBIA

VANCOUVER ISLAND

Strait of Georgia

VANCOUVER

Clayoquot
Sound

WASHI
STA

VICTORIA

0   50   100   150   200 kilometres

0   50   100 miles

USA

SEATTLE

In September 1990, my father Peter McAllister, co-founder of the Raincoast Conservation Society and former director of the Sierra Club for western Canada, organized a one-week reconnaissance voyage to the Koeye River. He chartered a three-masted schooner and invited bear biologists, photographers, journalists and environmentalists to come along. I was lucky enough to squeeze on board. I had just finished a season of treeplanting in the interior, and setting sail for a valley of grizzly bears seemed a refreshing change. When we headed north from Port Hardy, I knew as much about grizzly bears as I knew about photography—very little. By the end of the trip I still had not seen a grizzly bear, but what I had seen was in some ways even more captivating.

Everywhere in the Koeye valley there were signs of bears—where they had lain down in beds of moss under big old trees, and where they had walked on trails worn deep into the forest floor by hundreds of generations of bears moving between their favourite fishing spots and the cover of forest. The tracks of wolves and bears crisscrossed the riverbanks, and the soil of the estuary had been ripped apart by bears digging up roots. Out in the river the salmon were so thick it looked as if we could walk across the water on them.

One evening I sat on a piece of driftwood with my feet wrapped in the sand, staring out toward the open Pacific. Fitz Hugh Sound was calm as glass and it looked as if the sun was being lowered into the hollow of Hakai Pass solely for my benefit. The rear paw print of a grizzly bear lay fresh in front of me, intricately etched into the moist sand. Not only was I deeply impressed by the rare beauty and ecological significance of all that I was seeing, I was damn curious about what kind of animal went with a footprint so large.

I knew from that moment forward a large part of my time was going to be devoted to tracking that shy monarch of the rainforest, the maker of these great tracks, and trying to understand how its fate and the fate of the wilderness rainforest were joined.

On the return journey through Queen Charlotte Sound, everyone on board fell silent as the obvious question moved through us like electricity. If the Koeye River could be so spectacular and yet so unrecognized, what about the eighty or ninety other river valleys on the mainland coast that were still intact and unprotected?

A few months later, Earthlife Canada released a report that pinpointed many of the intact river valleys on the north coast, showing that almost a hundred remained wild, undeveloped and unprotected. By this time Karen was back from her own explorations of the Nass River and Haida Gwaii (the Queen Charlotte Islands), equally mesmerized by what she had seen. Together we studied Earthlife's maps, staring into a world full of bears and rainforest, a world we found irresistible. What were all those rivers like? Were they

Ian and Karen McAllister relax at Pooley Island, one of their favourite raincoast stops.

alive with salmon? What did their estuaries look like? What plants grew there? Did grizzly bears and wolves walk their banks?

Over the winter we collected as much information as we could about every dot on the map, scouring provincial and federal government offices and libraries. The information barely filled a shoebox. Clearly no one—no government and no private organization— had ever undertaken an inventory of this coastline in search of even the most basic biological and ecological information. Yet the rights to log the forests of these valleys had been licensed to large logging companies, a decision that would deface the wild raincoast landscape forever.

One night, with maps spread out across the floor, a few of us decided to begin exploring the river valleys of the north coast. My father Peter, Baden Cross, Cindy Lee (a photographer who had been on the first Koeye trip), Karen and I founded the Raincoast Conservation Society right then and there, and began making plans.

In 1991 we began a systematic aerial reconnaissance of all the intact river valleys between Bute Inlet and the Alaska border. Michael Humphries, a director of the Society, owned a small Cessna airplane and with a video camera mounted on one wing we flew up and down every single valley on the coast building a complete library of video and still imagery. Then a friend told us about a sailboat for sale in Ontario—cheap. We thought of how great it would be to sail our own boat and spend as much time as we could on the coast. So we bought the *Companion* over the phone, flew east that winter to pick it up, dropped it into Lake Ontario and set sail for the Panama Canal.

We started out knowing next to nothing about open ocean sailing, using placemats to navigate inshore waters and getting ourselves into and out of all kinds of trouble in offshore waters. By the end of the trip we were well versed in celestial navigation, had sailed through the waters of eight different countries, and had put 30,000 sea miles under our belt.

But even as we sailed along both coasts of North America and Central America, and then on to Hawaii, our hearts were always looking north toward the temperate rainforests of home. On our final leg homeward from Hawaii, as we were pushed along toward the north tip of Vancouver Island by the blustery northeast trade winds, a fog bank rolled down from the north, smothering all traces of wind. Suddenly the swells which had

The McAllisters' floating home and research station, the *Companion*, at anchor in the estuary of the Lockhart Gordon Creek near Rivers Inlet.

A rainforest research expedition of the Raincoast Conservation Society puts ashore in Dean Channel at a scenic little gem called Jump Across Creek.

been so gigantic only hours before calmed down to a barely detectable smoothly rolling sea. We couldn't see the front of the boat through the thick fog, but we could make out the distinct fragrance of kelp and cedar trees, and when the foghorn on Cape Scott sounded it brought tears to our eyes. These were the sounds and scents of home, and our next expedition was about to begin.

That first fateful trip into the Koeye taught me two things: that a river valley truly can change a person's life forever, and that I had better buy a camera. Since then, Karen and I have returned each year, along with other members of the Raincoast Conservation Society, charting and photographing the coastal river valleys between Knight and Portland inlets.

Now that we had our own boat we could spend as much as seven months a season doing research and photography. Our goal was to explore every single intact valley on the mainland coast, assessing wolf and bear populations as we went. This goal was finally reached in the spring of 1996, when we set foot in Smokehouse Creek off Smith Inlet, the last valley on our list.

During those years we have had the great privilege of learning the landscape, its waterways, its plants and trees, its large and small birds, fish, insects and mammals. In the later stages of our exploration many of the world's leading environmental groups began recognizing the global significance of what has now become known as the Great Bear Rainforest, and arguments for its protection began to be as familiar as those over South Moresby, the Clayoquot and the Tatshenshini were before those precious wilderness areas were saved.

The debate is unavoidable and necessary, but the problem is that the very values we struggle to protect sometimes become obscured in the verbal tug-of-war. Especially because British Columbia's northern coast is so little known, we want to place at least a sample of its indescribable natural beauty on the record so that all may have an opportunity to appreciate what is at stake. We have tried to include the basic information required to understand this vast and complex area, but our main purpose has been to express our own appreciation of it, in the wish that some of the joy it has given us might be shared, and some of our concern for its future might be shared also.

Princess Royal Island north of Bella Bella is world famous for its unique local strain of all-white spirit bears.

OPPOSITE Karen explores Waump Creek in Alison Sound, through a screen of branches festooned with epiphytic (tree-dwelling) plants.

16

ANCIENT FORESTS
of the SALMON BEAR

The morning dazzles and sparkles, the waters of Bond Sound shining with a rain-polished brightness after days of downpour. The cabin of our 36-foot plywood trimaran is steaming with drying socks, rain gear and wet camera equipment. The *Companion* has become so overrun with Karen's burgeoning plant collection that it feels more like an arboretum than a sailboat, and we are only setting out. This is our seventh annual journey up the northern BC coast to photograph and explore places where the ancient

Beautiful Ahta River in Bond Sound near Knight Inlet is one of the southernmost intact valleys in the Great Bear Rainforest.

19

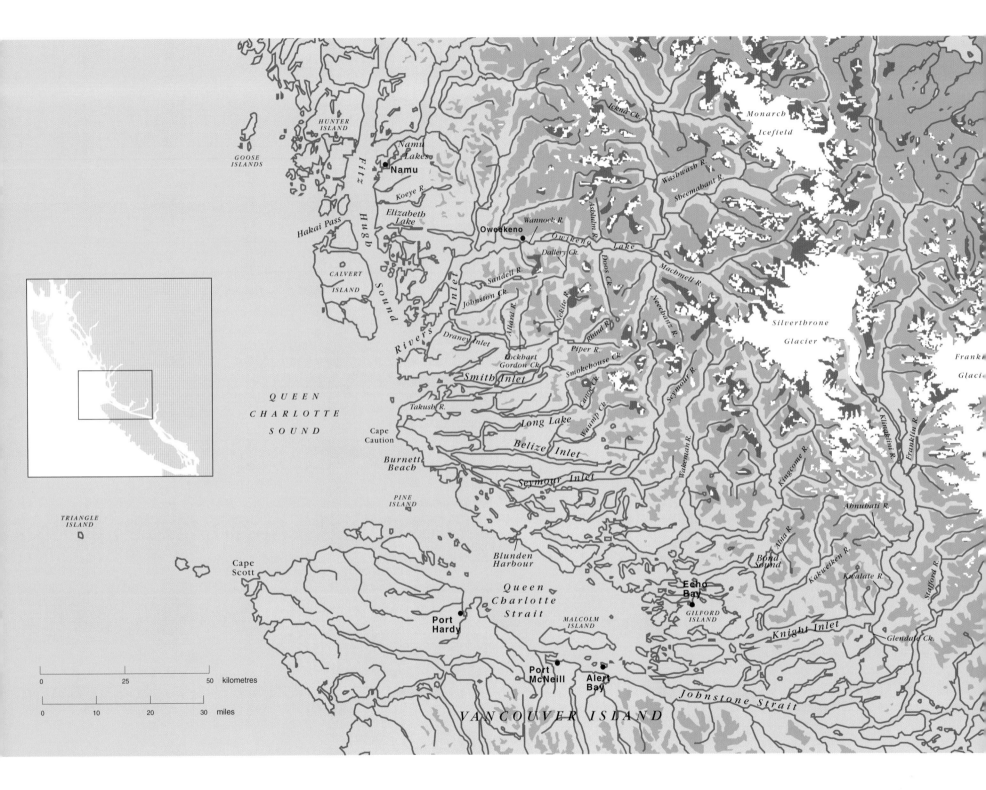

GOOSE
ISLANDS

HUNTER
ISLAND

Namu
Lakes

Namu

Koeye R.

Elizabeth
Lake

Fitz
Hugh
Sound

Hakai Pass

CALVERT
ISLAND

Oweekeno

Wannock R.

Owikeno Lake

Washsblini R.

Wasbwasb R.

Sheemabant R.

Monarch
Icefield

Ickna Ck.

Rivers
Inlet

Draney Inlet

Sandell R.

Johnston Ck.

Allard R.

Nekite R.

Dallery Ck.

Doos Ck.

Machmell R.

Neechanz R.

Silverthrone
Glacier

Frank
Glaci

Lockhart
Gordon Ck.

Smith Inlet

Piper R.

Rhind R.

Smokehouse Ck.

Takush R.

QUEEN
CHARLOTTE
SOUND

Cape
Caution

Canoe Ck.

Long Lake

Waump Ck.

Belize Inlet

Seymour R.

Wakeman R.

Kingcome R.

Franklin R.

Klinaklini R.

Burnett
Beach

Seymour Inlet

Abnubati R.

PINE
ISLAND

TRIANGLE
ISLAND

Cape
Scott

Blunden
Harbour

Queen
Charlotte
Strait

**Echo
Bay**

GILFORD
ISLAND

Bond
Sound

Ahta R.

Kakweiken R.

Kwalate R.

Stafford R.

**Port
Hardy**

MALCOLM
ISLAND

Knight Inlet

Glendale Ck.

**Port
McNeill**

**Alert
Bay**

Johnstone Strait

VANCOUVER ISLAND

0   25   50   kilometres

0   10   20   30   miles

20

rainforest still reigns supreme. We step onto the deck to see if the anchor has dragged in the overnight wind. The boat is surrounded by dozens of pairs of marbled murrelets that keep diving underwater, one after the other, probably looking for emerging chum fry. The murrelets stay under for about twenty seconds, then pop up like bubbles.

After leaving our winter tie-up near Victoria, BC, bound for a season in the Great Bear Rainforest, our first stopover on the way north is Knight Inlet, where a cluster of unlogged valleys dangle southward, making up a kind of tail on the Great Bear. This morning we are just north of Knight Inlet where the Ahta River enters Bond Sound, and in the early morning mist rising off the water, a flock of mew gulls appears like peace doves as they hover above the water. Nearby four great blue herons share a fallen log, stalwart and still amidst puffballs of the swirling mist.

We watch as two large, dark shapes emerge from the treeline. One grizzly bear is walking along the river; the other is heading out toward a spit. They seem to be moving toward each other and we anticipate trouble. But they turn out to be friends, probably siblings. They feed on the riverside sedges for a while, then wander off together, exploring the tideline.

The misty waters of the Ahta River, rich with drifting salmon eggs, attract a noisy party of bald eagles and mew gulls.

OPPOSITE An abandoned log dump near Franklin River offers Karen a panoramic view of mountainous Knight Inlet, its wild character still impressive after generations of logging. Knight Inlet is the southern-most location where it is still possible to protect a significant area of intact ancient temperate rainforest.

BELOW LEFT A look of concentration comes over the face of a sow grizzly bear as she "fishes by feel" among the schools of pink salmon surging up one of Knight Inlet's many creeks. Salmon may make up as much as 95 percent of coastal grizzlies' fall diet.

BELOW RIGHT Grizzlies will patiently spend hours sifting through streamside gravels for salmon roe.

Henry David Thoreau wrote that only that day dawns to which we are awake, and it describes exactly how we feel right now—filled with the uncomplicated joy of the moment, spotting our first grizzly bears of the season. Even better, we recognize the bears from our earlier trips here. They are old friends, and look to have survived the winter in good shape.

The moment feels so natural, so normal, that we have to remind ourselves of its significance. A hundred years ago you could have sailed into any coastal river mouth between Mexico and Alaska and found grizzlies foraging for food at the water's edge. Now Knight Inlet represents the southern frontier of the coastal grizzly bear population of western North America. The grizzly has been displaced from 99 percent of its original habitat in the lower forty-eight states, and more than 60 percent of its original range in Canada.

If it were simply a matter of one of nature's most magnificent creatures sliding toward total extinction, it would be alarming enough. But it is more than that. The disappearance of the grizzly bear follows the disappearance of the great North American wilderness, because the grizzly depends on wilderness to survive. Once any kind of development

Stepping into the forest anywhere on the northern BC coast, one is surrounded by the towering western redcedar, western hemlock, Sitka spruce and the several true firs known popularly as "balsam fir." Douglas fir, the leading commercial species of the southern BC coast, is rare north of Vancouver Island, although stands occur sporadically. The large conifers account for most of the rainforest's huge biomass, but hundreds of lesser plants give the forest community or biome its incredible biodiversity. Coralroot, a saprophytic orchid, is often found at the bases of large trees, obtaining nutrients from decaying organic matter. Underfoot, foamflower and bunchberry are two of many flowering plants that carpet the forest floor. Delicious Alaskan blueberry is the largest of its species, often found along stream banks. Vegetation varies only slightly from here to coastal Oregon, forming a remarkable 2,000-kilometre strip that represents two-thirds of the planet's temperate rainforest.

Bunchberry, an understorey plant common to the inner forest floor.

starts in an area, the grizzlies of the surrounding landscape are doomed, although it doesn't always happen overnight. Why the mightiest of North American predators should be so vulnerable to environmental degradation when its lesser cousin, the black bear, has proven so adaptable is something of a mystery, but it gives the grizzly special importance as an indicator species. We can look at grizzly distribution figures for the whole continent and get a good idea of what is left of that natural paradise that so enthralled Europeans when they first happened on the new world. We can go further by considering that grizzlies once ranged over Europe and parts of Asia and northern Africa as well, and using their numbers to plot the historic decline of natural wilderness values throughout a sizable portion of the northern hemisphere. But looking just at North American numbers, we see the grizzly population has fallen to a fraction of its original size, and a disproportionately high number of the survivors are squeezed into the narrow river valleys of the northern BC coast. Official BC government estimates place between 1,500 and 3,000 grizzly bears between Knight Inlet and the Alaska border, giving the Great Bear Rainforest some of the highest concentrations of grizzly bears—and some of the largest individual specimens—in North America.

These numbers confirm that this particular coastal strip is one of North America's few remnants of fully functioning rainforest wilderness. We can look at healthy grizzly populations and have confidence that the integrity of the coastal ecosystem is intact and that the 230 bird species, 68 mammals, and thousands of insects and microorganisms that make their home in the old-growth forest are also healthy. If the grizzly numbers start to go down, we can be sure those other less visible values are declining too. That is reason enough to focus worldwide attention on these bears.

In our seven years of exploring northern raincoast habitat and the grizzlies that live there, we have also become captivated by the bears themselves. We never tire of watching them, because each bear has a unique personality and because their relationship with the forest is so uncanny. At first the bears' massive bulk and heavy armament seem out of place in an environment so soft and spongelike, but the grace with which the huge creatures disport themselves among all this fragile complexity is a virtuoso performance we can't stop applauding. Sometimes on busy bear trails we find clumps of untouched wildflowers we swear they must be stepping around deliberately. Elsewhere, bears searching

The grizzly bears that use this relatively new "mark" trail almost seem to have gone out of their way to avoid stepping on the delicate pink fawn lilies that line it. These highly unusual trails, which are formed by successive generations of grizzly bears following exactly in each other's steps, are unique to the coast and are thought to mark the bears' territory.

25

Pristine rainforest environments like some areas of Knight Inlet provide ideal grizzly habitat, supporting some of the highest bear concentrations in North America.

BELOW Fish-bearing rivers of the northern BC coast still play a key role in the livelihood of coastal First Nations. Here Kwakwaka'wakw from Alert Bay ferment the smelt-like eulachon to produce a pungent fish oil or "grease" traditionally traded among coast and interior groups. Unlike salmon, eulachon spawn in springtime in just a dozen select rivers along the BC coast.

for root plants have ripped up estuary soils like bulldozers—which couldn't be better for the estuary. It is this many-faceted relationship between the bear and the forest that we have found our most rewarding study, and if we dwell on it, it is because we find it the most profound symbol of what this ancient ecosystem is all about.

IAN'S JOURNAL : I should have realized that the sudden flurry of gurglings and throaty cracks from the ravens above meant there were more life forms about than just me and the birds. Suddenly the devil's club and salmonberry bushes began to shake and I knew that within seconds huge claws would be digging into the mud of the well-worn bear trail where my gumboots were currently planted. I backed off to the side about twenty feet, trying to decide whether to run, yell, play dead or pray to God, and finally chose, out of confusion mixed with curiosity and fascination, to do nothing. I sank deep into the moss of an old spruce stump—bear spray in hand—and just watched as the big bear lumbered down the trail, nose up, and stopped in mid-stride right in front of me. We stared at each other across the sword ferns. Salmon blood stained his mouth and he seemed well fed. He did not seem alarmed at my presence. The look in his eyes when they met mine was one of gentleness, almost sentience. The claims of some of the less restrained bear experts that grizzlies can sense those who mean them harm suddenly seemed less fanciful—an impression that dozens of subsequent grizzly encounters have only confirmed. Then the 225-kilogram bear lowered his head and passed on without even snapping a twig, as beautiful as anything I have seen. It was, you might say, a watershed experience.

Heading up Knight Inlet we find ourselves in the middle of the spring migration of eulachon. A huge school of these smeltlike fish begins to accompany us, followed along by a parade of salmon and sea lions. A seething pod of white-sided dolphins run the eulachon up against the rocks just off our stern. This huge web of life will migrate to the end of Knight Inlet and up the Klinaklini River. Counts of two and three thousand eagles have been reported during the peak of the annual run, and the Kwakwaka'wakw of Alert Bay still fish the eulachon for its oil.

We finally reach the mouth of the Ahnuhati River, our destination for the day. River corridors like the Ahta and the Ahnuhati are the lifeblood of the raincoast. Every year their waters come alive with Pacific salmon swarming upriver to spawn and die, and these valleys are where the ancient forests and their understorey vegetation grow most

ABOVE Franklin Glacier in the rugged mountain wilderness behind Knight Inlet.

RIGHT The snow-capped mountains of the Coast range clearly separate the lush temperate rainforests of the Pacific coast from the dry interior plateau to the east. Many of these coastal peaks and ranges remain unexplored.

profusely, providing habitat for bears and other wildlife. Most of the forest valleys around Knight Inlet have been logged with only the Ahnuhati, the Ahta, the Kwalate and upper Stafford remaining intact. These four valleys taken together represent the most southerly location on the central and north coast of British Columbia where it is possible to protect a significant area of intact ancient temperate rainforest—some 112,000 hectares of coastal grizzly bear habitat.

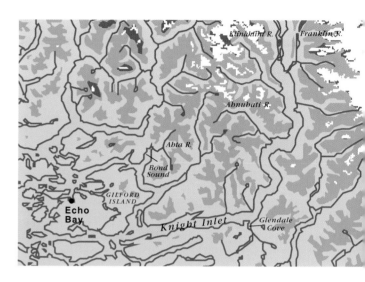

KAREN'S JOURNAL : Walking upstream on the left side of the Ahnuhati River, my feet sink in the fluid muck. There is a brief moment of panic when the first pull does not immediately yield my tender foot. I've read stories of Pacific quicksand, mud that doesn't swallow you up like in the tropics, but holds you 'til the tide comes in and drowns you. I try to walk more swiftly—less time to sink. It makes you realize how convenient it is for grizzlies to be equipped with four such barge-like feet.

Soaring high above the Ahnuhati, a turkey vulture glides with the midday thermals in a distinctive V-shaped pattern. This is the vultures' most northerly range and our most southerly. A part of us would be content to go no farther than this one valley, to stay and really get to know the cycle and inner workings of one system, but we have a lot of miles to sail and rivers to walk before the winter closes in. We prepare a late dinner and settle in to read by the kerosene lamp. As an evening breeze rattles the main halyards against the aluminum mast, we reflect on how Knight Inlet has been stripped of much of its wilderness character, yet how it is just too rugged a landscape to be completely tamed. The last thing to be done tonight is to tune in to the forecast for tomorrow's weather, because with any luck we will greet the new day by sailing on the open Pacific.

THE GREAT BEAR RAINFOREST IS ENCIRCLED by a ring of outer islands which are for the most part only lightly forested and have a very different ecology from the inner islands and fiords. The most extreme outer island ecology of all can be observed on treeless Triangle Island, which juts out of the Pacific like the dorsal fin of a giant shark 50 kilometres west of Vancouver Island. Of all British Columbia's outer islands, this one withstands some of the most extreme weather conditions. On the island's summit hunches the base of an old lighthouse that became a maritime legend when some of the worst storms ever experienced on the BC coast forced the Canadian lighthouse service to abandon the site in 1920, leaving Triangle "to the uses for which nature apparently designed it at the beginning

Virtually free of terrestrial predators, isolated Triangle Island is one of the rare places where bald eagles nest at ground level.

ABOVE Oystercatcher; young elephant seal.

LEFT The ecosystems of outer coastal islands are very different from the protected inner islands of the coastal rainforest. Triangle Island, which has no trees, is a bird sanctuary used for nesting by hundreds of thousands of birds.

31

of things." That use turns out to be providing refuge for some of nature's most defenceless creatures. Today the precipitous green slopes are one massive nesting ground.

For the sheer density of nesting birds, there is nothing to compare with Triangle Island anywhere else on the BC coast—or, for some species, anywhere else in the world. Some one million birds nest here in the course of a year, largely because Triangle is nearly free of natural predators. Thirty thousand pairs of tufted puffins, a million Cassin's auklets (about 40 percent of the world's population), 84,000 rhinoceros auklets, and more than 10,000 common murres are among them. The biologists working on the island tell us that numerous pairs of rare Peale's peregrine falcons live there.

After spending time among the deep, dark fiords of the mainland with their immense forests full of bears and wolves, it is hard to get used to a place so open to the elements, but our initial impression of barrenness soon gives way as we find our senses bombarded from all directions. Pods of sea lions occupy every beach and rock that we can see. Cliffs encrusted with brilliant orange lichen tower over a bed of false lily-of-the-valley. A tagged fox sparrow buzzes by and a small harem of elephant seals rests near the water's edge. Gazing upward, we see six sandhill cranes soaring high on the thermals above the island. Just then, a small falcon flies toward the cranes, knocking one of them out of formation. The crane falls in a mess of feathers, before regaining its composure and rejoining the other five as they fly higher, away from the island. The pelagic cormorants are beginning to build their nests, and the gulls seem to coexist peacefully with all the nations of birds. The tidepools are rich in anemones and the starfish are decorated in a multitude of shimmering capes and shiny ribbons of seaweed. It is a miracle that the bird droppings that fall from the sky like giant hailstones fail for so long to nail us. When a puffin flies overhead and treats Karen to a guano shampoo, we take it as our cue to leave.

OPPOSITE As many as 30,000 tufted puffins live on Triangle Island.

ABOVE RIGHT A trio of roaring female Steller's sea lions presents an impressive deterrent to any nearby males who might harm the young pup. Recent Alaskan studies show Steller's sea lion numbers are diminishing so rapidly, northern populations may be extinct in fifty years.

BELOW RIGHT In 1920 some of the worst storms ever experienced in BC caused the Canadian lighthouse service to abandon Triangle Island to the elements.

FOLLOWING PAGES Having sailed northward from Knight Inlet out of the shadow of Vancouver Island, the Companion lies at anchor off Burnett Beach, Cape Caution.

CONTINUING TOWARD THE CORE OF THE Great Bear Rainforest, we next venture upon the broad stretch of Queen Charlotte Sound—a lengthy crossing that exposes small boaters to the full fury of the open Pacific as they thread their way up the Inside Passage. We press onward to Cape Caution, a point of land that can strike terror into the heart of even the most experienced mariner. Making this journey is like a rite of passage we have to endure if we are to be granted entry into the core of the raincoast. Most boats catch a window of calm weather and pass through here without a backward glance; others still lie torn and fractured beneath the cape's rocky headland. Today we slide by wave-washed Pine Island light station, the fog enveloping us in a hypnotic greyness, speckled only by guillemots and murrelets that rest with ease on the smooth waters. Life seems to be unfolding in slow motion, but it is hard to relax when you're out on the Sound. Even after more than thirty crossings, we never know when the spirits of the open ocean will rear up and try to swallow us in a tide rip or smash us on one of the Sound's countless unseen reefs.

Once past Cape Caution we enter the waters that form the broad mouths of Smith and Rivers inlets, approaching an extensive region that might be thought of as forming the haunches of the Great Bear. It is a landscape that is still a stronghold of coastal wildlife—

Pacific white-sided dolphins often swarm up the inlets of the raincoast in great numbers, entertaining boaters of the Inside Passage with their acrobatic antics.

LEFT Looking west down Owikeno Lake and Wannock River into Rivers Inlet. Though tragically diminished in recent years, this drainage was once one of the greatest sockeye salmon producers in the world.

OPPOSITE The outer coast of the Great Bear Rainforest is rich with intertidal life.

including grizzly bears—despite an extensive history of development. These inlets hold a prominent place in local lore owing to the huge runs of highly prized sockeye salmon that once spawned in their headwaters. All five of the major Pacific salmon species—chinook, coho, pink, chum and sockeye—hatch in the gravel beds of the many creeks and rivers, swim out to sea for a period of two to seven years, then return to spawn and die in the waters of their birth. But the sockeye, whose rich red meat has long made it the most lucrative commercial species, is unique in that after hatching it must spend one year or more in a freshwater lake before it is ready to head out to sea. On the whole coast there are only a few places with the right conditions for sockeye, and both Rivers and Smith inlets have them. The tremendous sockeye stocks gave rise to a canning gold rush in the late nineteenth century, and twenty-one large canning complexes sprang up along the inlet shores between 1882 and 1937. By 1996 just a few ruins remained, dilapidated and crumbling back into the sea, and there was not a commercial fish boat in sight.

The gleam disappears from the eye of a chum salmon after it returns from the open Pacific to spawn and die in the small rainforest stream of its birth. The survival of its race will depend on the forest watershed retaining enough ecological integrity to purify, regulate and cool rearing waters.

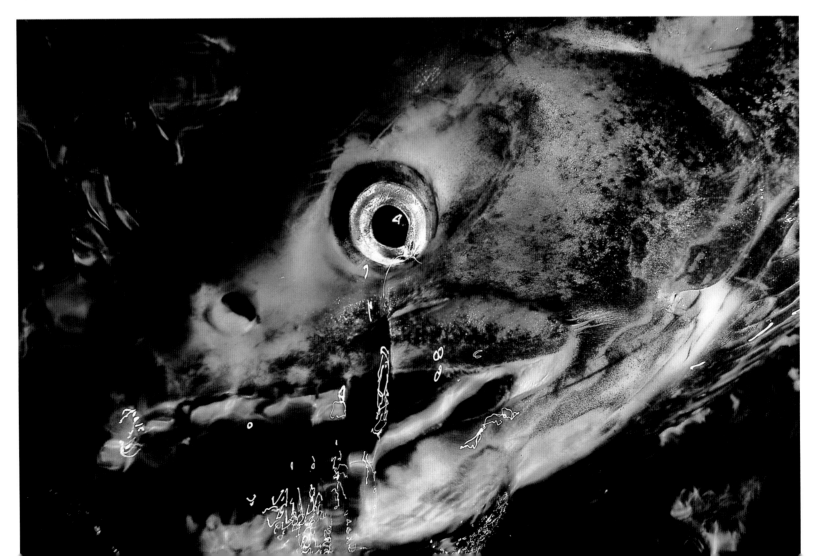

ABOVE Gulls are one of many species that thrive when salmon runs are abundant.

LEFT The slumping remains of Wadham's Cannery, one of more than twenty canning complexes built to exploit the salmon wealth of the Smith Inlet-Rivers Inlet region between 1882 and 1937. Like other resource industries on the northern BC coast, salmon canning has come and gone leaving little but ruins.

Overfishing had something to do with the decline of the runs, but in 1968, eleven years after the last cannery closed, Rivers Inlet could still muster a healthy return of 3.2 million sockeye. The real turnaround came after the government chose, over the protests of major fishery and First Nations organizations, to permit clearcut logging in the salmon-bearing watersheds around Owikeno Lake at the head of Rivers Inlet. With the same doggedness that drives the tobacco industry to insist smoking doesn't necessarily cause cancer, the forest industry insists clearcut logging doesn't necessarily harm salmon stocks. But critics are unanimous that removal of the forest cover in this steep, rain-washed country inevitably causes uncontrolled runoff to damage spawning beds and rearing waters. The indisputable fact is that after twenty-eight years of clearcutting, the once mighty Rivers Inlet sockeye run fell from over 3 million fish to 65 thousand, and one of the planet's great salmon fisheries had to be closed to commercial harvesting. This folly reflects a fact of life that in BC the forest industry is king, and has the political clout to bulldoze its way over all other interests, even those of other big industries.

Despite the long history of logging in the Rivers Inlet–Smith Inlet region, wild rivers like the Waump, Smokehouse, Takush, Lockhart Gordon, Piper, Allard, Sandell, Johnston and Dallery still survive the chain saw and give the area's fugitive wildlife some prime rainforest habitat. The Takush Valley, lying on the south side of the entrance to Smith Inlet,

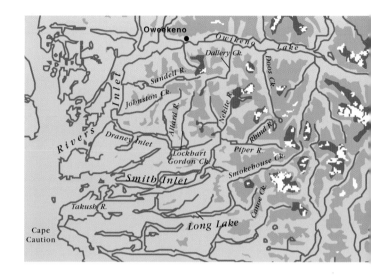

OPPOSITE Sockeye salmon spawners in Dallery Creek, one of only two intact sockeye-producing watersheds left in the Owikeno Lake system. Since clearcut logging began around the lake, the once great sockeye runs of Rivers Inlet have declined from a high of 3 million to a low of 65,000.

LEFT The Rivers Inlet basin is fed by more than twenty creeks and rivers, each fed in turn by numerous tributary streams which may support their own runs of salmon. Protecting the genetic diversity of the coast's innumerable smaller runs could well hold the key to the long-term survival of the species.

is a rare form of rainforest—influenced by the wind and weather of the rugged outer coast, yet possessing all the qualities of a protected valley hiding away in the back of an inlet. A First Nations village site here was occupied by the Gwa'sala people until the 1960s. It would have been a good place to live, so handy to the marine riches of the outer coast, yet secure in the quiet waters of the protected inner coast. Today the site is covered in salmonberry bushes, but the thick layers of shell midden (refuse heap) bear witness to centuries of past occupation.

On the mudflats we hide behind an uprooted cedar tree and watch four wolves in front of their den. We watch them in a misty rain for five days. They seem to hang out around the den all day long, then in the evening bound up the river into the forest, where they disappear for the night. One evening our curiosity overrides our better judgement, and when we think the adults are gone we approach the den. There, at the base of a weatherbeaten redcedar, we see a little mound of grey pups. One about the size of a nerf football disentangles itself from its siblings, wobbles bowleggedly over and lets out a pint-sized snarl. When we fail to retreat in terror, he wobbles back to his siblings and resumes chewing on an old deer jawbone. A moment later a low, throaty growl erupts to our left, and we know that this is no pup, but a full-grown mother none too happy about what she sees. This time we do retreat, hearts in our throats.

On our last morning in the Takush, before we leave for Smokehouse Creek, we go to watch the wolves one last time. They see us, and seem to have accepted us as long as we don't pull any more stunts. A sudden loud booming sound shakes us all alert. The wolves stand up and look toward the valley where the sound still reverberates. Six Canada geese rise up honking. The wolves circle uneasily, a younger one nipping at the largest one's ear. They are obviously disturbed by this strange unnatural sound. The adults circle a few times and halfheartedly respond to the playful gestures of the younger members of the pack. Then they return to settle down again on the green carpet of new grasses, casting cautious glances up the valley. From where we sit, we can see signs of roadbuilding, the source of the dynamite blasts. International Forest Products will soon be logging the Takush.

The trip to the Smokehouse is one we have put off for years. With camping gear piled high in leaky dry bags, we run the inflatable 40 kilometres to the back of Long Lake, an unrelenting sleet pelting the narrow slits of our eyes. Awesome cliffs rear up before us, and water tumbles in chutes from peaks we can't see the tops of. We peer through the rain at granite bluffs where blurred pictographs of fish, coppers, people's faces and a dozen canoes making their way to the mouth of the river remind us that, adventurous as we feel, others have been making this soggy trip for thousands of years.

OPPOSITE **A pack of gray wolves relaxes in the estuary of the Takush River, Smith Sound. The northern BC coast has high concentrations of wolves, which are legally hunted with a limit of three per hunter.**

Pink fawn lilies.

Rock paintings or pictographs bear witness to long occupation of the coast by First Nations peoples. The shield-like figures above are a rare depiction of ceremonial coppers, a traditional medium of wealth, while the unusually clear and realistic composition below shows seagoing dugouts travelling in formation.

OPPOSITE In spring flood, the heavy forest cover surrounding the 38,000-hectare Smokehouse Creek drainage acts as a giant filter and reservoir, controlling heavy runoff and preventing harmful siltation of salmon beds. Located at the head of Long Lake off Smith Inlet, the Smokehouse remains one of the largest unlogged producers of sockeye salmon on the coast.

The Smokehouse is in flood, making it appear Amazonianly vast. Tall Sitka spruce trees stand along the water's edge. The last time Ian flew over Long Lake the water was a glacial blue and fringed with sandy beaches. Now there isn't a metre of shore on which to pitch a tent. Sitka spruce more than 2 metres in diameter seem to rise all around us like cathedral spires. For the next few days we spend our time observing the world from the tops of hemlock or young spruce trees, waiting for the grizzly bears to make their appearance.

KAREN'S JOURNAL : A grizzly pokes his nose out of the bush and is surprised to come face to face with a girl who is answering the call of nature. Ian was looking in the other direction and when he turned around the bear had galloped off. Ian was annoyed I had frightened the poor bear away, but I thought it was me who was in the most vulnerable state. It was quite decent of Mr. Bear to allow me the privacy of a pee.

From the tall ridges surrounding the head of Long Lake we can look down into Smokehouse and Canoe creeks, the Waump to the south and the Piper and Rhind rivers to the north. These valleys form the southern terminus of a large contiguous central section of the Great Bear Rainforest that extends 200 kilometres north all the way to the Kitlope Valley—far on the other side of Bella Coola. The Waump watershed, which is just over the mountain from where we perch in the Smokehouse, actually empties into Alison Sound in the next inlet system down the coast, a circuitous 150-kilometre boat trip to the south. It is a delightfully tangled-up territory.

It has taken us several years of sailing in and around the river valleys of Rivers Inlet, Smith Inlet and Owikeno Lake to begin to understand that each river is unique, and that the valleys are like pieces of a jigsaw puzzle, each one part of a larger picture. The Nekite River and its tributaries tucked in at the head of Smith Inlet play an important role as a travel corridor for grizzly bears that move from the Smokehouse and Waump watersheds in the south, to the Lockhart Gordon Creek and Owikeno Lake to the north. Each river valley has its own special habitat that grizzly bears rely on. For instance, a grizzly bear that was born in the Johnston Creek Valley will learn from its mother about the better foraging sites—in the estuaries of the Lockhart Gordon and the Nekite in the early spring, then the skunk cabbage patches of the Doos Creek Valley, and in late summer berries on the hillsides of Allard Lake. Most important is the bears' intimate and precise knowledge of the timing of salmon runs, from the Johnston with its early run of pink salmon in July, to the nearby Dallery and Smokehouse with their late runs of sockeye. It is this knowledge, coupled with unrestricted access to food sources, that remains the key to their survival there.

Heading back to the entrance of Smith Inlet, we are pushed along by a pleasant out-flow wind. We sail through a short distance of exposed water, and then we are in Rivers Inlet. We poke our way into the narrow mouth of Draney Inlet and head toward Lockhart Gordon Creek, an unlogged 12,000-hectare valley at the back of the inlet. Scars left behind by recent logging along the way make the pristine Lockhart Gordon seem like a hostage in its own land.

One of the remarkable features of the Lockhart Gordon is its exceptionally large estuary. If a river has a heart, the estuary is it. Here, where land and sea come together, life is at its most abundant. The bears eat the sedges that proliferate, Canada geese raise their young and migratory waterfowl use it as a staging area. The sheltered waters protect salmon fry from seals, birds and other predators. Wolves and raccoons dig up clams and other mollusks.

One valley north of Draney Inlet is Johnston Creek, called "Hole in the Wall" by locals, and as we approach it from the inlet, that's all it looks like. But farther up, past a boulder garden of tumbling rapids and deep coho salmon pools, we come upon a breathtaking serpentine river system weaving its way through chest-high sedges. An extensive rain-forest covers the valley, which is crisscrossed in every direction with bear trails. Large runs of pink and coho salmon have made the Johnston an important grizzly bear valley. We have heard of people seeing nine grizzly bears at a time at the mouth of the creek.

OPPOSITE Though Ian and Karen try not to compare one raincoast valley with another, the Lockhart Gordon Creek is one of their favourites. Even from the air you can see the trails of its many resident grizzlies weaving through the sedges. Broad estuaries like this one also play a critical role in the life cycle of the Pacific salmon, providing clean, protected, nutrient-rich rearing waters for juvenile fish.

A male grizzly feeds on Lyngby's sedge, a dietary mainstay of many coastal grizzlies. The bears spend more time eating plants than meat and rely on the vegetation found in coastal estuaries during the spring and early summer, prior to the fall salmon runs.

Many of the drainages in Rivers Inlet have been logged and some local salmon populations have been destroyed in the process. In 1997, the Johnston Creek remained intact and was one of the most prolific producers of both coho salmon and grizzly bears, but logging plans by International Forest Products put both at risk.

IAN'S JOURNAL :   The trail up Johnston Creek is muddy going at the best of times, but this is October and the trail is a quagmire. It is my third time back to the valley this year and I know as I work my way through the mud that it could be my last chance to see the valley intact. With a canoe and a sixty-pound pack on my back, I am too focussed on the mud, which I am slowly sinking into. Suddenly I hear that all-too-familiar long hissing sound grizzly bears make when you piss them off.

I try to assess the situation in order to react appropriately, like they tell you in the bear attack books, but I just can't recall an example in which an aggressive mama grizzly is huffing and puffing her way toward an individual with his legs entombed in mud and a canoe on his shoulders. I know this is not a false charge. I utter something foul, incoherent and very loud, and plunge face first into the mud, bringing the canoe down on top so it encapsulates me. Millions of years from now, I think, archaeologists will be digging through this site and find the bones of a crazed-looking being with a canoe on its head. But I am lucky. The mother decides I am not worth troubling over and leaves me in my red plastic shell.

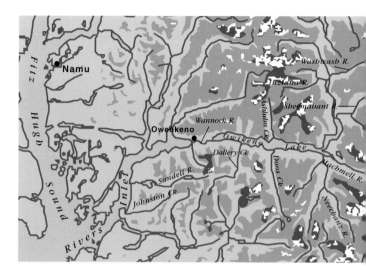

We continue up Rivers Inlet to the community of Oweekeno (pop. 60), which sits on the edge of the Wannock River separating Owikeno Lake and Rivers Inlet. The Wannock River is a torrent. There's no way we can get our trimaran through so we tie up at the village dock that floats in front of Oweekeno's one street. On our way to the band office we meet Frank Hanuse Sr., one of the band councillors and fisheries wardens for the village.

"I want to go south this winter and get my conservation officer's ticket," Frank says. "Then I can spend more time on the problems facing our bears back up the lake." He nods upriver, and we ask him what problems he means. "Poaching, and hunting. They just found another subadult grizzly with its parts ripped out in the Ashlulm. The hunters fly in and fly out and we are left with nothing but dead bears."

At that moment a fully loaded logging truck rumbles through the edge of the village. Frank looks up at it, and then over to the river where some salmon can be seen pooling up. He comments on how the Oweekeno have such limited access to salmon these days, and how all the trees seem to be leaving their region. "That is our history and our future being stolen from us," he says. "The government considers us a third party in decision making and we are left beggars in our own land."

As we work our way up the Wannock River to Owikeno Lake in our Zodiac, we watch a subadult brown and silver grizzly bear half swimming, half walking in front of the houses perched alongside the river. The logging trucks continue to rumble along the banks, hauling away the old-growth rainforest that once flourished in the network of river valleys surrounding the lake.

We motor to the back of the lake past the first, second and third narrows and find one spot that is not scarred by logging. At the mouths of the Inziana and the Sheemahant rivers we examine cabins that sheltered decades of trophy hunters. Notes scrawled on the walls boast of bear kills made over the years, and we are amazed at the some of the sizes claimed. In the early 1960s, when the nature writer Andy Russell came to Rivers Inlet to photograph grizzlies, the bears' wary habit of feeding at night made him think they had become conditioned to avoid trophy hunters. "I suspect that a great many more bears had been killed than the population and annual increase would support," he wrote. The surrounding landscape was once some of the best grizzly bear habitat in the world, and it seems obvious why. No other part of the BC coast had so many salmon-producing rivers in such a concentrated area.

Official and public indifference to the loss of irreplaceable local fish stocks like some of those in Rivers Inlet is something that has always baffled us. In BC, according to the American Fisheries Society, 766 stocks of salmon are either extinct or at high risk of extinction. When a local stock is extinguished, all the genetic specialization that it developed over thousands of years of adapting to that particular location is lost. Meanwhile, local wildlife populations such as grizzly bears, which require the rich supply of fish

Rivers Inlet grizzly hunters relax at a cabin on the Inziana River once used by the legendary Nuxalk guide Clayton Mack. Through the 1990s, the legal hunt took about 350 BC grizzlies each year. Hunters are supposed to target older males, but 50 percent of recent Rivers Inlet kills were female.

The surge of rich food provided by fall salmon runs allows the coast's dense population of grizzlies to survive winter hibernation, but bears are not the only beneficiaries of the salmon. Eagles, ravens, wolves, otters, raccoons, squirrels and a host of forest creatures share the nutrient wealth of the spawning salmon, fertilizing riverside vegetation with their waste. In the river gravels, decaying salmon carcasses nurture a universe of micro-organisms that will in turn nourish hatchling fish. When even a small salmon run is destroyed by logging or overfishing, this web of rainforest life is broken.

OPPOSITE The glacier-green waters of Wannock River at the outlet of Owikeno Lake is the site of Oweekeno village, the ancestral home of the Oweekeno people.

fat and protein to survive winter hibernation, are also reduced or destroyed. With grizzlies, substantial reduction often means extinction, because their reproductive rate is so slow a local population cannot rebound after numbers are seriously reduced. The average sow produces only eight cubs over her twenty-year lifetime, and will not mate if food is scarce. This is one of the reasons world grizzly numbers are in steady, long-term decline, and why the northern BC rainforest is one of the grizzly's most important holdouts.

Local riverside flora are no less dependent on the salmon. Bears and other predators distribute the salmon carcasses and nutrient-bearing waste up the banks, stimulating plant growth. As Fisheries consultant Jim Lichatowich says, "The salmon is the one animal that penetrates the whole northwest ecosystem, from the mountaintop where the eagle takes the carcass to feed its young, all the way out to the Japanese current in the Pacific."

The Rivers Inlet example is key to concerns many people have about the future of the northern BC coast. Studies show destructive practices such as large-scale clearcutting, yarding logs across streams and cutting to the water's edge were still being routinely approved by the BC government in 1997, and if the coast's remaining intact watersheds are subjected to this kind of treatment, it may be facing its last days as one of the world's richest nature refuges.

The refreshingly intact Dallery Creek is located about 16 kilometres from Oweekeno Village on Owikeno Lake. When we first arrive, our expectations for viewing grizzly bears aren't very high, so when we round a bend and see five young bears standing in the creek we feel very lucky indeed. We are struck by one of the grizzlies in particular, a dark male with long silver patches along his back. We nickname him Silversides and watch him turn up stones and gravel, looking for beds of freshly laid eggs in this sockeye spawning ground. Eventually the other four bears leave, but Silversides merely nods in our direction as he takes over one of the vacated fishing spots. He stands so still that the only motion we detect is a barely perceptible sniffing, then all of a sudden he springs into action. Quicker than you can blink an eye, he has a salmon in his mouth. There is no rhyme or rhythm to his eating frenzy, which is simply an instinctive preparation for the long winter ahead. Sometimes he consumes every last part of the fish, other times he lets it wriggle around for a few seconds and then drops it back in the water. But mostly when he bites down on a fish he sends streams of pink eggs flying most delightfully into the air, then fastidiously licks up every wayward egg from nearby rocks. He is very much in his own world here, and we can only hope that he has a full life ahead of him.

CHAPTER TWO

INTO *the* HEART
of the GREAT BEAR RAINFOREST

J ust north of Rivers Inlet lies the main body of the
Great Bear, a vast coastal wilderness region rich in
old-growth trees and teeming with wildlife. We
return here year after year to explore the countless
channels, inlets and islands that lie between Fitz Hugh
Sound and Seaforth Channel, and to sail the long fiords
all the way to the base of the Coast Mountain range.

On the map showing the remaining ancient temperate
rainforest in British Columbia, this region stands out in

A vast archipelago of unbroken rainforest surrounds the Heiltsuk community of Waglisla
(Bella Bella), forming the heart of the Great Bear Rainforest.

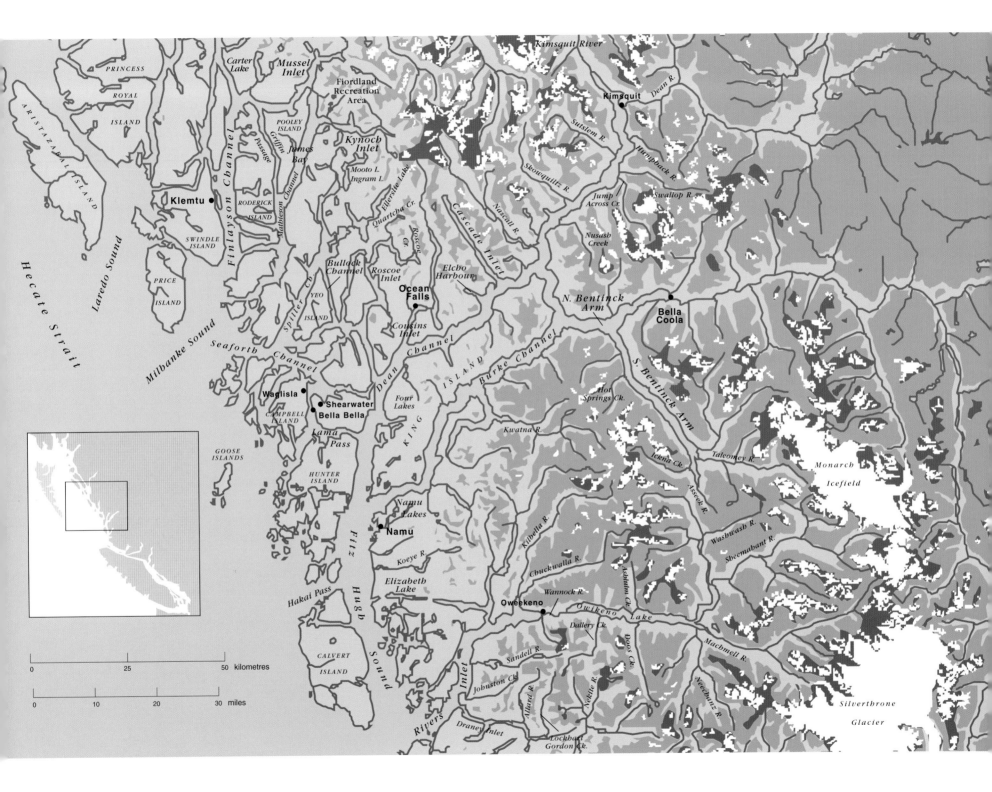

PRINCESS ROYAL ISLAND

Carter Lake

Mussel Inlet

Kimsquit River

Fiordland Recreation Area

ARISTAZABAL ISLAND

POOLEY ISLAND

Kynoch Inlet

Dean R.

Kimsquit

Sutslem R.

Mooto L.
Ingram L.

Skowquiltz R.

Humpback R.

Griffin Passage

James Bay

Klemtu

Finlayson Channel

RODERICK ISLAND

Mathieson Channel

Ellerslie Lake

Quartcha Cr.

Roscoe Cr.

Cascade Inlet

Nascall R.

Jump Across Cr.

Swallop R.

Hecate Strait

SWINDLE ISLAND

PRICE ISLAND

Spiller Ch.

YEO ISLAND

Bullock Channel

Roscoe Inlet

Elcho Harbour

Nusash Creek

Laredo Sound

Milbanke Sound

Seaforth Channel

Ocean Falls

Cousins Inlet

Dean Channel

N. Bentinck Arm

Bella Coola

Waglisla

Shearwater
Bella Bella

CAMPBELL ISLAND

Lama Pass

Four Lakes

KING ISLAND

Burke Channel

Hot Springs Ck.

S. Bentinck Arm

GOOSE ISLANDS

HUNTER ISLAND

Kwatna R.

Ickna Ck.

Taleomey R.

Aseek R.

Monarch Icefield

Namu Lakes

Namu

Kilbella R.

Washwash R.

Koeye R.

Chuckwalla R.

Ashlulm Ck.

Sheemahant R.

Fitz Hugh Sound

Elizabeth Lake

Wannock R.

Oweekeno

Owikeno Lake

Doos Ck.

Machmell R.

Neechanz R.

Hakai Pass

Sandell R.

Dallery Ck.

CALVERT ISLAND

Johnston Ck.

Nekite R.

Silverthrone Glacier

Rivers Inlet

Draney Inlet

Allard R.

Lockhart Gordon Ck.

0   25   50 kilometres

0   10   20   30 miles

solid green: twenty-five of the thirty-six river valleys here are intact. But none of this wilderness is protected and it seems that everywhere we turn, we encounter fresh examples of development sprouting like a rash across the wild landscape.

Cradled between the mainland and Calvert and Hunter islands, Fitz Hugh Sound is the main route to Alaska, part of the fabled Inside Passage and a major intersection for water traffic on the central coast. Boats collect here before being funnelled eastward up Burke Channel to Bella Coola, or westward through Lama Passage to Bella Bella.

Hakai Pass separates Calvert and Hunter islands, and directly opposite the pass on the coastal mainland, with a view of the open Pacific, are the long sandy beaches that mark the mouth of the Koeye River—the place where our quest to know this fogbound part of the coast was born.

The canopy of the rainforest is its own crucible of life, where thousands of species of microbes, arthropods and other organisms thrive in the epiphytic plants that drape the branches of the old-growth trees.

Archaeologists have proven some ten thousand years of human habitation in this labrynthine archipelago. Dozens of Nuxalk, Oweekeno and Heiltsuk ancestral villages once thrived here, among them a community of Koeye people at the mouth of the Koeye River. Years ago, when their village broke up, some of the families went north to Namu and Bella Bella, and the others went south to Oweekeno. Today both the Heiltsuk to the north and the Oweekeno to the south claim the 18,625-hectare Koeye watershed as part of their ancestral lands.

Signs of the human past are barely detectable now; they are fast becoming a part of the rainforest. Even a limestone quarry and its outbuildings, only a few decades old, are beginning to crumble and dissolve into the beach. And all that remains of one old homestead nestled back in the trees are a few decaying cedar fenceposts.

Fallen cedar longhouse beams are all that remain of a once important Kwakwaka'wakw village at Blunden Harbour, one of hundreds of First Nations settlements that dotted the raincoast a century ago. Today most evidence of the aboriginal past has dissolved into the forest.

ABOVE Near the Takush River, Karen examines an old-growth cedar tree with a scar showing where Gwa'sala people long ago removed a slab, probably for a house plank. The western redcedar, which spread across the rainforest landscape only 4,000 years ago, provided First Nations people with light, strong, easily worked wood of massive dimensions ideal for making dugout canoes, longhouses and totem poles. Clothing was also woven from the stringy bark and baskets were made from the tough roots.

LEFT A support post carved in the likeness of a bear presides over the site of a vanished longhouse near Waglisla.

What has endured are the deeply indented grizzly bear trails that cross the valley. Four species of salmon run up the river and edible plants carpet its bountiful estuary. When their internal tide tables let them know the tide is out, Koeye bears wander down to the beaches to feed on crabs, mussels and other shellfish, an integral part of their diet.

IAN'S JOURNAL : It took me three hours to work my way up the Koeye estuary this morning, standing downwind of the occasional inflows from Fitz Hugh Sound. The sun, somewhere beyond the mist, is brightening up the estuary. About 175 metres across the main channel a large dark female grizzly is feeding near the treeline with three fat yearling cubs. Watching through my binoculars, I can practically hear the sedges grinding in her teeth and the gentle tearing of root mat as she dexterously separates the gritty silt and humus to reveal small clusters of starchy rice root. Her cubs closely watch her every move.

Every fifteen or twenty seconds her huge head jolts up, and with her mouth still full of sedges she stops chewing. Her nose is covered in muddy silt and she works one nostril at a time—forcing them into the wind, she smells the world around her. I feel somewhat devious for being downwind. A nagging part of her tells her to beware of me, but her nose calls the shots and she cautiously resumes eating. I kick some rice root with my boot and out pop the little white shells. Through the binoculars I can see the family of bears getting fat on a food source the size of a marble.

The danger for the Koeye grizzlies now is that their valley is quickly becoming isolated from adjacent landscapes. Natural boundaries surround the Koeye on three sides—Rivers Inlet to the south, Burke Channel to the north and Fitz Hugh Sound to the west. The only route the grizzlies can take in and out of the valley runs right through Tree Farm Licence 39, and MacMillan Bloedel holds the rights to log it. Clearcuts are already encroaching on the Koeye valley from all sides, and roadbuilding has started in the adjacent Cold Creek valley.

Eight kilometres north of the Koeye is the traditional Heiltsuk fishing village of Namu, one of the most ancient sites of human habitation on the northwest coast. Archaeologists have found its middens contain almost ten thousand years' worth of shells and artifacts,

A grizzly bear might spend hours in an estuary digging up the roots of the rice root lily.

OPPOSITE When food is plentiful, a mother grizzly can give birth to three—or even four—cubs in the same year. Grizzly bear cubs are remarkably small at birth, measuring 20–25 centimetres in length and weighing half a kilogram.

After winning a temporary reprieve from logging in 1990, the beautiful Koeye River valley near Namu fell victim to a resort development that reduced the white sand beach to a quagmire of stumps and diesel slicks. Since recreational activity has increased, observers have noticed a significant decrease in grizzly bears using the Koeye estuary.

Kayaker exploring the Koeye River.

providing clues to what this place was like when glaciers still dominated the landscape and the rainforest was just beginning to evolve. In 1893 the prehistoric site took a whole new direction when a cannery was built there, and Namu remained an important commercial fishing centre until the late 1960s, when changes in fish packing technology made it redundant.

It is almost dark when we tie up to the old cannery dock at Namu, and although the pilings look as dilapidated as they did when we were last here four years ago, a freshly painted "cafe—open" sign reminds us we'd heard someone was trying to revive the place. We jump into our "town" clothes and rush up the ramp, only to find that there is indeed nothing open. The cafeteria door is ajar, but the only sign of life is a cat scrounging in the kitchen. Newspapers, dirty coffee cups, napkin boxes and menus sit on every table. Down the street, clipped hair still litters the floor of the abandoned beauty salon.

Namu, like Butedale, Ocean Falls and so many other resource communities that have flourished and died on the northern BC coast, continues along its way to becoming another unsightly ruin, adding to the chain of collapsed cannery buildings, ghostly smoke-stacks, abandoned dams and hazardous rotten pilings that punctuate this part of the coast. The logging operations have come and gone even more quickly, leaving their vastly greater scars. Of the dozens of canneries, pulp mills, logging camps and mines started in the area

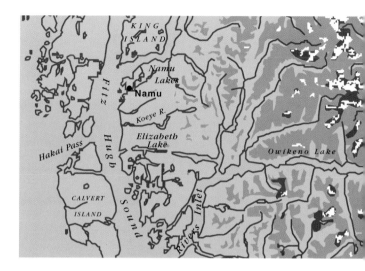

BELOW LEFT Archaeological excavation site in Namu, documenting at least 10,000 years of continuous habitation.
BELOW RIGHT Until recent times, Namu was the busiest canning and fish packing centre between Vancouver and Prince Rupert.

63

River otters are among the many forest creatures for which spawning salmon provide a dietary mainstay.

OPPOSITE Even after death, the Pacific salmon continues to contribute to the rainforest ecosystem, reaching even to the mountaintops where the eagle carries the fish carcass to feed its young.

in earlier years, not a single one survives. Only the First Nations stay on to keep faith with the land. A visitor can't look upon the woeful legacy of resource exploitation on this frontier—so much aggressive invasion and so much harmful disturbance followed by so much pathetic retreat—without questioning what it finally achieves.

We walk up to Namu Lake where we spot a cougar loping down the beach. It looks large, even from a distance, as it blends with the tawny backdrop of the sand. We are downwind but note the keen-eyed feline still turns to check us out before slipping into the woods. We hear a lot about cougars and the bounty that used to be on their heads, but we seldom actually see one.

Back at the dock we have the good fortune of bumping into John Lewis, one of the few federal Department of Fisheries & Oceans (DFO) patrollers working the central coast. John's job is to make sure the commercial fishing fleet complies with regulations. It's also his job to walk up every fish-bearing stream in his patrol area, literally counting the fish as he goes. That's how people in his position come to be called "creekwalkers." John was up in these parts counting fish five years before we were born. We ask him about this season's salmon run. "Worse than last year's," he says, "and worse than the year's before."

Individual salmon runs on the BC coast continue to have their ups and downs, but there has been a pattern of general decline for many decades. Rivers Inlet is the most dramatic example, but unfortunately not the only one. The Canadian government favours intensive enhancement of large runs in selected river systems like the Fraser and Skeena, but people like John believe the key is to conserve all the coastal salmon stocks, especially the thousands of tiny, apparently insignificant runs that find their way into so many small and nameless creeks. When we ask him whether there is any hope for the fishery, he doesn't need much time to think it over. "As long as two fish survive, there is hope," he says. Noting our expressions of dismay, he adds, "And of the opposite sex, of course."

KAREN'S JOURNAL : Today I walk along the shores of a river full of salmon, whose every strand of being is focussed on procreation. I jump toward the river, and the salmon detect my shadow and scatter. *Gorbuscha, nerka, keta, kisutch* and *tshawytscha*: these are the species names of Pacific salmon—Russian names—and I think about the land bridge over which so many creatures travelled to this new continent, where perhaps only the salmon were familiar.

Some scientists believe that salmon locate their birthplace by smell. I take a deep breath, and I am able to tease out an odour of damp earth and decaying leaves. Is that what they smell?

Bella Coola, at the head of North Bentinck Arm, is the only community between Kitimat and the Powell River area linked by road to southern BC.

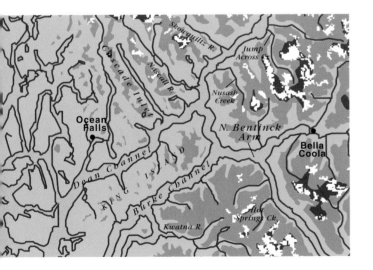

Sailing north from Namu and bearing right, we enter Burke Channel and head northeast toward Bella Coola. The forests of King Island loom over us to the northwest, and we watch a pod of exuberant orca whales circle the island in search of salmon. We have heard stories of people seeing sixty or more whales in Burke Channel at one time, when two or more orca pods come together.

White granite bluffs line the upper inlet as we move deeper and deeper into the Coast range, which begins to feel like we are entering the interior of British Columbia. Bella Coola, a combined white and First Nations settlement of some 3,000 people at the head of North Bentinck Arm, is 100 kilometres inland from the shipping lanes of the Inside Passage. This is Nuxalk territory and, until the nineteenth century, the site of an aboriginal nation with thirty-seven villages in the productive valleys of the Bella Coola, Dean, Kimsquit, Skowquiltz, Asseek, Taleomey and Kwatna rivers. Bella Coola is the only west coast settlement between the Vancouver area and Kitimat that can be reached by road from the other side of the Coast Mountains.

The Bella Coola region also has a long history of logging in valleys of the region's major rivers. Today only a few small intact river valleys remain in Nuxalk territory, three of them—Ickna, Hot Springs and K'iskwatsta creeks—on South Bentinck Arm. The remaining ones are part of a cluster of valleys on the north and south sides of the upper Dean Channel.

Logging is a contentious issue within the Nuxalk community. Some depend on it for much-needed jobs, others oppose it on principle. In 1995 several Nuxalk people travelled to King Island to stand in front of bulldozers that were poised to push through a logging road for International Forest Products (Interfor). In a confrontation that lasted several weeks, three Nuxalk hereditary chiefs and several non-Native protesters were arrested. The protest and the trial that followed helped focus world attention on the fundamental question of whether logging should be allowed in remaining old-growth forest, not just in Nuxalk territory, but throughout the northern coast of British Columbia. In the summer of 1997, logging was reopened on King Island and the Nuxalk chiefs once again invited environmental groups to join them in their campaign to protect their ancestral lands.

ABOVE   Orca whales often follow salmon migrations up raincoast inlets deep into the Coast range.

LEFT   First Nations petroglyphs adorn the shoreline rocks along Dean Channel.

The 29,000-hectare Skowquiltz valley is the jewel of the Dean Channel. With its unlogged forests and an expansive estuary that unfolds at low tide like a massive green blanket covered in sedges and grasses, the Skowquiltz has the makings of the perfect grizzly bear valley. But in the heat of summer we wonder if Skowquiltz isn't another word for horsefly. Karen claims that the prospect of an attack by "these ghastly beasts" weighs more heavily on her mind than a grizzly bear attack.

KAREN'S JOURNAL : Ian darts off to the other side of the estuary where he has spotted a black bear. I see him peering over the top of a fallen spruce, but when I next turn my eyes toward the bear, it has disappeared. Then I look back to where Ian should be, but he has disappeared as well. I wander across the shallow flats to where my friends have so neatly vanished, and what do I hear emanating from the woods but Ian in conversation with— well, something. So I too fade into the brush, where I find Ian gazing skyward, still in deep discussion. It occurs to me that all those years his mother sent him to Catholic schools have finally paid off, but I should have known better. Looking up, I find the object of his devotion is no radiant light, but a dark, furry, roman-nosed *Ursus americanus* (black bear), who seems to be quite comfortably lounging on a wide spruce bough about 3 metres off the ground.

Unlike grizzly bears, black bears are relatively abundant in BC—population estimates range from 63,000 to 160,000. A black bear requires less food than a grizzly, has a higher reproductive rate and can adapt to a variety of habitats. About 4,000 black bears are legally killed by hunters in BC every year, compared to about 350 grizzlies. Another 800 black bears and 50 grizzlies are killed by conservation officers each year, usually because the bears are attracted to garbage dumps and become too aggressive around people. The number of bears killed illegally is open to speculation.

IAN'S JOURNAL : It rained so hard last night even the bears are depressed. Just yesterday their gait was brisk and they consumed fish with great abandon. Today the gloom has gotten even to them. They mope about the estuary at half stride, heads low, listlessly cuffing the occasional spawned-out chum carcass.

Heading on down Dean Channel back toward the outer coast we pass the aptly named Cascade Inlet, with its umpteen waterfalls tumbling down from 24 kilometres of snowy peaks, then Elcho Harbour where the nearby Mackenzie monument commemorates the

Although black bears are more numerous than grizzlies in most parts of the BC coast, they tend to be less territorial and avoid straying into the prime habitat of their larger cousins.

OPPOSITE Clouds and mist act as permanent blankets over the rainforest, moderating temperatures and holding in the dampness. Sometimes even in midsummer the day comes and goes without a hint of a ray of sunshine. With its rich rainforest and expansive estuary, the intact Skowquiltz is the jewel of Dean Channel.

western terminus of explorer Sir Alexander Mackenzie's historic journey across Canada in 1793. Fifteen kilometres farther on we pass Cousins Inlet, which for sixty-five years boasted the largest settlement in these parts, a pulp mill town of 5,000 known as Ocean Falls. Ocean Falls was famous for two things: its phenomenal 4,350-millimetre yearly rainfall, and its impressive roster of Olympic medal-winning swimmers, who used to say they had an edge because they could practise their backstroke while walking to school. Closed in 1982, the mill is now on its way to becoming the largest industrial ruin on the coast, but a small determined community of people live there and the old hydro plant now supplies power to Bella Bella.

IAN'S JOURNAL : Wisps of mist float through the raincoast year round. Even in midsummer the misty light of day can come and go without leaving a clue that such a thing as the sun exists. The sun has no fixed time of arrival or departure; instead it fades in and out like the tide, from dark to grey to dark again. Everything in the landscape is constantly wet.

The coat of the grizzly bear has evolved to shed the water, but the conifers have evolved to collect it. I have watched the mist drift freely over a stripped mountain until it comes to a line of

ABOVE **The pulp mill that gave Ocean Falls its reason for being was closed in 1982, but a small and growing community still lives on the site.**

RIGHT **The oversize leaves of the devil's club allow it to thrive in the low light of the deep rainforest, making it one of the prominent understorey species. Its red berries are a favourite food of the grizzly.**

OPPOSITE **On the raincoast, you either learn to enjoy the wetness or move to the desert.**

ABOVE The marten and the blue grouse are two of the approximately 300 wildlife species that inhabit the BC temperate rainforest.

RIGHT Because its decorative, rot-resistant wood makes it ideal for roofing, siding and finishing, western redcedar has long been one of the most prized commercial tree species in the rainforest. Notches in the trunk show loggers started in to fell this giant before the days of chain saws when the huge trees were taken down using axes and hand saws. Why this job was left half done is a mystery.

standing timber, then it holds up as the trillions of needles catch the droplets and feed the trees. One old-growth conifer can hold some 19,000 litres of water.

The raincoast is made of water and water gives it life. Here in the heart of the raincoast, up to 5,000 millimetres of rain falls every year, but it comes at you in every form—dew, mist, fog, spray, sleet, snow, all of it feeding creeks, rivers, waterfalls and lakes. The moisture retainers such as trees and moss have their work cut out slowing it all down so it doesn't just carry the whole place away. Up here you either fall in love with wetness or move to the desert.

Bella Bella is the catchword coastal travellers use to describe what is really a group of three villages: Old Bella Bella, Shearwater, and New Bella Bella or Waglisla. The largest is

Tim McAllister, Ian's brother, walks an inflatable up the Nascall River, a spectacularly scenic but little known watershed in the Dean Channel south of the Skowquiltz River.

Waglisla, a modern First Nations village of 1,200 people on the east coast of Campbell Island. With the demise of Ocean Falls, Waglisla and Shearwater are now the main supply depots for small boat traffic on the central coast. Waglisla is the headquarters for five Heiltsuk tribes and home to a school, a hospital, an airfield, a BC Ferries terminal, a community college extension and a fish processing plant run by the Bella Bella band.

Despite the trappings of modern life, some ancient themes persist in Waglisla, none more prominent than the historic relationship between people and salmon. Walking through town, the fragrance of smoking salmon wafting from backyard smokehouses seems ever present. In the evenings, families barbecue salmon over open fires, some of it to be canned and stored on pantry shelves. Marge Housty, a Heiltsuk friend, has often shown us her rows of jars and cans of salmon prepared in half a dozen different ways. "It's like collecting firewood," she says. "We are always a few years ahead in our supplies. Plus, my father prefers the taste of the salmon on its fourth year."

There is no road here—the Bella Bella area can be reached only by air or by water. Perhaps this is why, when we first sailed into the islands of the Heiltsuk people, we felt

BELOW LEFT Heiltsuk life today is a study in contrasts, with the modern and the traditional continuing side by side. Here fresh sockeye are barbecued in the old way, over an open fire.

BELOW RIGHT Heiltsuk workers participate in the global economy using the latest in fish processing technology to process chum salmon roe for export to Japanese sushi houses.

as if we were sailing back in time. Much of the west coast of Vancouver Island and the southern mainland must have looked just as these islands do when Captain Vancouver and his crew sailed through two centuries ago.

If a rainforest as vast and diverse as the Great Bear can have a heart, then this region must be it. The forests that surround Roscoe Inlet, Yeo Island, and Ingram, Mooto and Ellerslie lakes lie at the centre of the largest contiguous block of intact temperate rainforest in the world. This intricate rainforest archipelago is defined less by individual river valleys than by islands, coves, lakes, creeks and channels. Hundreds of creeks drain down into the inlets, and although each one is small, together they make up one of the most diverse repositories of salmon stocks remaining on the coast. Each creek is home to its own unique race of fish, different from that of even its closest neighbour. On a coast where wild salmon have to compete with introduced species and resist new diseases, the diversity of these micropopulations of salmon may well hold the key to the survival of the species.

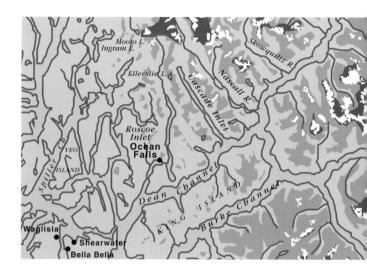

The unmarred wilderness of the Inside Passage makes it one of the world's most popular cruise ship routes. Here the SS *Westerdam* passes Waglisla.

FOLLOWING PAGES Aerial view over Ingram, Mooto and Ellerslie Lakes (at right) and Roscoe Inlet (at left) vividly shows how the northern BC coast is dominated by granite escarpments and ecologically unproductive high country. Less than 7 percent of the landscape supports productive low-elevation rainforest that nurtures the rich biodiversity of the Great Bear Rainforest.

Remains of a black-tailed deer that was unable to outrun a pair of hungry wolves. There are thought to be about 8,000 wolves in BC, with some of the highest concentrations occurring on the northern coast.

Rainforest trees continue to play an important role in the ecosystem decades after they fall. Here a decayed trunk or nurse log provides an ideal site for new growth.

IAN'S JOURNAL : In Bullock Channel, I watch a pack of wolves traverse the tidal flats in search of deer, or a seal or a dolphin washed up on shore. Two of the larger wolves spot a deer on the opposite shore. They pace back and forth at the tideline, their steamy breath coming in short bursts, considering the long cold swim across the channel. Then finally they plunge in. One wolf reaches the beach about a half mile down from the deer and the other lands about the same distance above it. They enter the forest and close in. The hapless deer is still foraging on leafless huckleberry bushes when suddenly she realizes what's happening and makes a run for the water. Karen and I have often watched deer outswim wolves in close matches, but this time the race never even begins. The small deer barely touches the water before the wolves are on her back. As soon as she feels their weight, she stops struggling. A deer is born with the knowledge that a wolf will always be close behind.

Fishing is still the leading employer in Waglisla, but logging has a growing influence. The old-growth forests of the Central Coast Timber Supply Area have been parcelled out to a few large forest companies on long-term tenures. Almost all the forests covering the northern portion of Heiltsuk territory and the Kitasoo lands farther north are controlled by Western Forest Products. By the early 1990s the company had logged much of its old-growth forests on Vancouver Island and was increasing its activity on the northern coast. Its new logging camp on Yeo Island just a few miles north of Waglisla, signalled that the

A key characteristic of the coastal temperate rain-forest is its mild winters. Low-elevation snow and ice, like that seen here in Ellerslie Lake, is the exception.

Longtime Waglisla resident and teacher Larry Jorgenson is a storehouse of knowledge about the territory surrounding Ingram, Mooto and Ellerslie lakes and Roscoe Inlet, which is steeped in Heiltsuk history.

OPPOSITE The ancient temperate rainforest of British Columbia is a moss-draped, mist-shrouded forest built on ecological foundations that took 10,000 to 14,000 years to evolve—a unique combination of plants and animals that in turn migrated here from ecosystems as old as 70 million years. Growing slowly but virtually year-round in the wet, moderate climate, the ancient trees can endure for a thousand years or more, contributing to a total forest mass (biomass) of some 1,000 tonnes per hectare— exceeding that of tropical rainforests.

lands surrounding the village, so long untouched, were soon to develop the mangy appearance so familiar on the southern coast.

Nothing in Heiltsuk territory brings conflicting values to the fore so sharply as Ellerslie Lake and its two associated lakes, Ingram and Mooto, 48 kilometres north of Waglisla. In addition to being one of the great beauty spots of the coast, the area is a vault full of legends and history, pictographs and traditional medicines of the Heiltsuk people. Since time immemorial the Qvuqunyaitxv ("calm water people") hunted mountain goat, fished and found spiritual solace in these lakes before moving to Waglisla.

We first explored the lakes in 1991, not knowing anything about them except that Western Forest Products had plans to log them. We were equally impressed by their scenic splendour and a cigar-chomping local character we discovered lounging in front of a fishing cabin in the far reaches of Ellerslie. This was one of the lake system's most devoted fans, a teacher from Waglisla named Larry Jorgenson, and he was even more surprised to see us than we were him. He told us we were the first people that he had seen come into the lake in fifteen years, aside from some Ocean Falls pilots who dropped in occasionally to fish.

It was a fateful meeting. Over the next few years Larry and his family became good friends and helped us in the effort to raise awareness about the endangered lakes. Round River Conservation Studies from Utah has now completed watershed assessments of the area, a rediscovery cabin has been built to focus on traditional teachings, and a bighouse healing centre is in the works. At the insistence of the Heiltsuk people, Ellerslie Lake was granted a deferral from logging plans, but Ingram and Mooto remain symbols of threatened rainforest values on the northern coast.

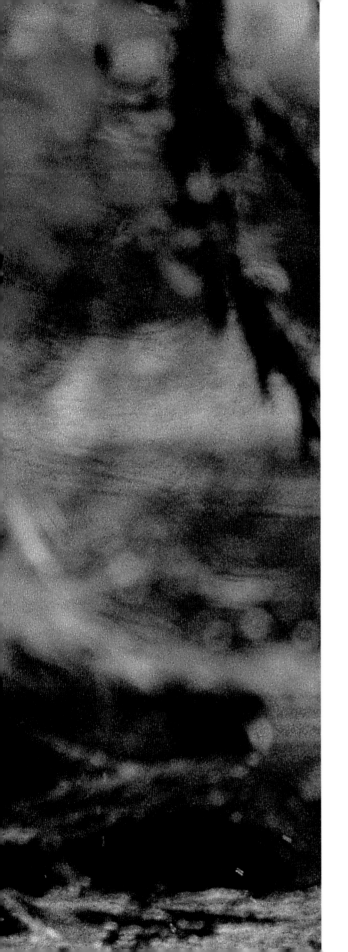

CHAPTER THREE

AMONGST *the* FIORDS

Seaforth Channel, north of Bella Bella, marks the shift to a very different raincoast landscape. The low-lands give way as the Coast Mountains swoop closer to the shoreline. The outer coast is a maze of islands, channels and inlets, and on the protected mainland, some of BC's most spectacular river valleys radiate from Mathieson and Tolmie channels. To navigate these waters is to pass through long, dramatic, seemingly endless fiords and to cruise by mountains that soar straight

Spirit bear, Princess Royal Island.

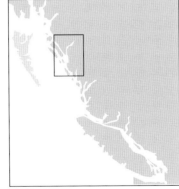

Kitimat R.

Kitimat

Kitamaat Village

Giltoyees Inlet

Jesse Lake

Foch R.

Kildala R.

Devastation Channel

Quaal R.

Douglas Ch.

Sleeman Ck.

HAWKESBURY ISLAND

Kitkiata Inlet

Crab L.

Brim R.

Owyacumish Ck.

Kemano R.

Hartley Bay

Gardner Canal

GRIBBELL ISLAND

GIL ISLAND

Kitlusb R.

Kiekiane R.

Aaltanbash R.

Princess Royal

CAMPANIA ISLAND

Butedale L.

Koeussas R.

PRINCESS

Khutze R.

Kitlope R.

ROYAL

Yule L.

Green R.

Surf Inlet

Canoona R.

ISLAND

Green Inlet

Mussel River

Kimsquit R.

Caamano Sound

Carter L.

Mussel Inlet

Poison Cove

Laredo Inlet

Tolmie Ch.

Fiordland Recreation Area

Hecate Strait

ARISTAZABAL

Sheep Pass

Ki.

Sutslem.

POOLEY ISLAND

Pooley Ch.

Kynoch Inlet

Finlayson Channel

Grith Passage

James Bay

Mooto L.

Ingram L.

Skowquiltz R.

ISLAND

RODERICK

Ellersife L.

Quartcha Ck.

Niseall R.

Klemtu

ISLAND

Mathieson

Roscoe Ck.

Cascade Inlet

SWINDLE ISLAND

Laredo Sound

Roscoe Inlet

PRICE

YEO

Ocean Falls

ISLAND

Spiller Ch.

ISLAND

Dean Channel

Milbanke Sound

Seaforth Ch.

KING ISLAND

Burke Channel

Idol Point

Waglisla

Shearwater

Four Lakes

Bella Bella

Lama Pass

Kwatna R.

Fitz Hugh Sound

HUNTER ISLAND

Namu Lakes

GOOSE ISLANDS

Namu

Grenville Channel

PITT ISLAND

Lowe Inlet

BANKS ISLAND

Principe Channel

| 0 | | 25 | | 50 | kilometres |

| 0 | 10 | 20 | 30 | miles |

84

out of the water to a height of 1,000 metres or more. Getting anywhere takes time and patience, plus a strong tolerance for rain, wind and rough seas. Until now, the very inaccessibility of the region has been its best protection, and large sections of it are still undeveloped.

From Milbanke Sound, just past the Idol Point light, a series of channels fan out into the landscape, and they simply beg to be explored. We sail northeast, up Mathieson Channel, which will take us to Fiordland Recreation Area. But before we can reach Fiordland, we stop at Pooley Island quite by accident when the outflow winds that run south down Mathieson Channel force us to turn into James Bay for cover. Four days later we don't care what the wind is doing out in the channel. We never want to leave.

KAREN'S JOURNAL : Each watershed is completely different from the last, and after years of sailing the north coast I feel privy to the special signature carried by each creek. In this land of trees, it seems that green is all you see, but there are myriad colours for those with the eyes to see them.

The bright fall colours of the Pacific crabapple stand out in sharp contrast to the infinite shades of green of the rainforest.

ABOVE Because the marbled murrelet needs old-growth forest to survive, it is one of those species like the tailed frog, the Queen Charlotte Island goshawk, the lung lichen, Vaux's swift and others which are classed as "old-growth dependent." The galaxy of interdependent relationships in the ancient rainforest may well hold the key to such mysteries as why old growth is less vulnerable to disease and pests than managed timber stands, but scientific study is still in its infancy.

RIGHT Though old and lame, this gray wolf is able to survive in the favoured conditions found on Pooley Island.

OPPOSITE Few areas of the world can match the wildlife riches of Pooley Island, where Karen and Ian have watched wolves, grizzly bears, black bears, and a spirit bear feeding on the large pink salmon runs—all in the same day. James Bay (shown here) was about to be logged in 1997.

On Pooley Island, lakes and bogs and meadows are splattered across the interior, and enclaves of towering Sitka spruce lie hidden and sheltered by rocky outcroppings and granite bluffs. James Bay Creek supports runs of coho, pink and chum salmon and we have counted three wolf packs on the island. As well, we have watched a white spirit bear share a salmon stream with a grizzly. Black bears (of which the spirit bear is a rare variation) are better adapted to small islands than grizzly bears, but when the salmon are running, grizzlies don't hesitate to swim over to the island. These small inlets and channels are crossed every day by grizzly bears, deer and wolves.

KAREN'S JOURNAL : Ian was walking toward a black rock when suddenly it moved. Then he noticed a lot of black rocks. Around the same time he realized he had walked right into a sleeping wolf pack, one black rock stood right up and walked toward him, staring him in the eye. It was a large wolf, possibly older, quite thin and with a gimped leg. There were two younger wolves and a few pups around. They seemed unafraid. Ian took a few pictures but he was so excited he was shaking, and eventually they moved on. The next morning we snuck up on their den through the trees but they were not to be found.

One morning the silence is shattered by a helicopter landing nearby. It brings forestry engineers from the new logging camp on Roderick Island owned by Western Forest Products, whose Tree Farm Licence includes much of Pooley Island. Our dismay over

86

their logging plans is not relieved when they dismiss this storehouse of rainforest riches as "marginal timber" that will provide only two or three years' worth of logging. To us, the fact that the north coast is now one of the last places on earth where ancient rainforest values of this quality can be observed, elevates its worth beyond the calculable. To the loggers it is just a lot of scrub timber they would never bother with if they weren't driven to it by dwindling timber supplies down south. This puts the plight of the whole Great Bear Rainforest in a nutshell, and underlines how much our struggle is one of values. If only these men and their masters could enlarge their value system to register a tenth of what is really here, they wouldn't dream of trampling this masterpiece of wild nature for a bit of "marginal timber."

The encounter, like a hundred before it, recharges our determination to create wider public awareness of the real values at stake here before they are exchanged for a handful of wooden nickels.

The northeast tip of Pooley is part of the Fiordland Provincial Recreation Area, a 76,512-hectare, roughly oval tract encompassing Kynoch and Mussel inlets. Fiordland is a spectacular maze of estuaries, salmon rivers and granite-walled fiords which was designated following a BC government study in 1983. Logging is not permitted here, but as in most provincial parks and recreation areas, hunting is.

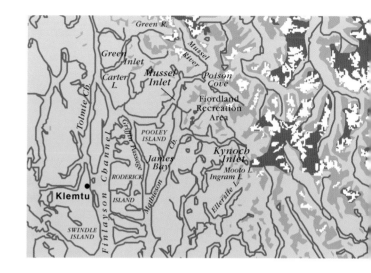

LEFT The towering ramparts of Kynoch Inlet loom through the mist, dwarfing the raincoast research vessel *North Star of Herschel Island*.

OPPOSITE Tim McAllister looks down into Kynoch Inlet where Ian and Karen's trimaran, the *Companion*, appears as a tiny white speck. The 76,512-hectare Fiordland Recreation Area offers some of the most spectacular scenery on the raincoast although it contains a minimum of productive low-level ground capable of supporting full rainforest biodiversity.

TOP While grizzly hunting is allowed in most BC parks and recreation areas, it is illegal to build permanent hunting blinds like this one near Mussel River.

BOTTOM This chalky skeleton is the remains of a grizzly bear shot by a hunter in Fiordland Recreation Area, possibly the female Karen had watched feeding here the previous fall.

OPPOSITE Grizzlies absorbed in feeding make easy targets for hunters.

One morning we sail north into the stunningly beautiful Mussel Inlet, off Mathieson Channel. We anchor our boat in Poison Cove and follow the salmon up Mussel River for several hours. As we wander along one of the well-worn bear trails, we come across a bear-hunting blind lashed to four small trees about 6 metres off the ground in a perfect spot to observe grizzly bears feeding in the stream below. Hunting may be legal here, but permanent blinds are not. We resolve to report it to the Ministry of Environment later, and to tear it down ourselves if, as usual, they fail to do anything about it. In the meantime it offers such a good chance to get close to some bears in total safety, we decide to get our sleeping bags and spend the night there ourselves.

KAREN'S JOURNAL : I sit in my treetop perch, alert to every noise that might indicate a bear is about, imagining a grizzly traipsing out between two grand cedar trees, wearing a garland of angelica and followed by an entourage of squirrel, deer and raven. I drift off listening to the evening chorus of songbirds and the pounding of salmon on the water, then open my eyes to find a grizzly right beneath me. She is medium-sized by grizzly standards but with her big belly full of salmon and the powerful mound on the back of her neck, she is the largest female bear I have ever seen. When she stands up on her hind legs and languidly rubs her back on the tree I can just about reach out and scratch her between the ears. Then she drops to all fours, scoops up a salmon, and inside of just a few minutes, she eats two or three more. Then she disappears into the berry bushes across the river.

Although the Wildlife Branch of the BC Ministry of Environment, Lands and Parks acknowledges that the grizzly bear population in British Columbia is at risk over the long term (blue-listed), they continue to support the legal hunting of approximately 350 grizzlies a year. The allowable kill is based on two assumptions: that about 4 percent of the bear population can be killed each year without destabilizing it, and that there are 10,000 – 13,000 grizzly bears in BC. The Branch admits its population figures are only "best guesses" and in fact had been estimating only 6,500 prior to 1990 when they "recalculated" the figure to 13,000. Some wildlife experts say the real grizzly population in BC is no more than 4,000 – 6,000. Since we know so little for sure, and a 1995 Angus Reid poll found 91 percent of British Columbians opposed to trophy hunting of bears, continuing the legal grizzly kill is one of those government actions that seems to defy logic.

OPPOSITE The world-famous Inside Passage with Princess Royal Island at left and the old cannery town of Butedale visible at top centre. Together with adjacent watersheds, Princess Royal is proposed as a spirit bear, grizzly bear and wild salmon refuge.

Klemtu, the only place you can call a settlement between Milbanke Sound and Douglas Channel, sits in the lee of Swindle Island. It is shared by two cultures—the Kitasoo people, from the Coast Tsimshian to the north, and the Xaixais from the south. In the last century, Klemtu residents made their living mostly by fishing, and by working at the canneries in the area, including a local one that operated between 1927 and 1968. It remains a strategic stop on the Inside Passage.

Just north of Swindle Island lies Princess Royal Island, at 230,000 hectares the fourth largest island in BC. The landscape here is quite different from the steep fiords of the mainland just 20 kilometres away. Much of Princess Royal Island is covered with low-lying scrub forests and numerous lakes of all sizes. But in the more sheltered river valley bottoms are stands of ancient forest where white bears and black wolves feast on the many runs of salmon.

Princess Royal Island is most famous for its local strain of white bears variously called

ABOVE The old way of catching salmon on the raincoast—the remains of a stone fish trap constructed by First Nations people long ago.

RIGHT Modern-day Klemtu kids load up on chum and coho salmon by casting high-tech "buzz bomb" fishing lures from the village boardwalk. Over 300 Kitasoo and Xaixais people make their home in the small Swindle Island community.

spirit bears, ghost bears and Kermode bears. For all its arresting appearance, the spirit bear is biologically no different from a black bear except that it carries a recessive gene for white or creamy white colouration. Its parents and siblings are typically black, and the whiteness characteristic surfaces in about one of every ten births on the island. Currently, ten to twenty white bears are thought to live on Princess Royal. White bears have also been spotted on Pooley, Roderick, Gribbell and other neighbouring islands, and on the mainland as far north as Terrace and as far south as the Kwatna River in Burke Channel. It is now illegal to hunt the famed white bear, but the island's black bears—some of which will produce white cubs—are not protected. In cooperation with the Kitasoo people, whose traditional territory includes Princess Royal Island, the Valhalla Wilderness Society has been working since 1989 to have Princess Royal Island, Pooley Island and the adjacent mainland coastal watersheds protected as a white bear, grizzly bear and wild salmon refuge.

One of a corps of fisheries patrollers known as "creekwalkers," Doug Stewart and his colleague Stan Hutchings monitor about 120 salmon spawning systems between Princess Royal Island and Douglas Channel. Most of Doug's creeks run clear but he is bracing himself for growing habitat damage as logging activity increases.

The white spirit bear or Kermode bear is a genetically unique member of the black bear family. Spirit bears are only found on the north coast of British Columbia, with the largest concentrations occurring on Princess Royal Island and adjacent islands, as well as in some nearby mainland valleys.

Raincoast grizzlies prefer to make their dens under the relatively open canopy of the old-growth forest, usually in the root cavities of large trees, and almost always above the freezing level where they are able to avoid torrential winter rains. Ian found this example while hiking above Green Inlet.

OPPOSITE Grizzly bears spend six months or more in hibernation, sleeping out the worst storms of the winter.

FOLLOWING PAGES Lined with tall stalks of devil's club, the pristine valleys of the Khutze (shown here), Kiltuish, Green and Aaltanhash river valleys are prime salmon and bear habitat.

The mainland across a narrow channel from Princess Royal Island is cut through with a series of forested creek and river valleys. From south to north Carter Lake, Green River, Yule Lake, and Khutze, Aaltanhash and Klekane rivers form the longest continuous line of intact river valleys found on the mainland coast of BC—and possibly the most scenic.

When we hike into the high country behind Green Inlet, the southernmost of these valleys, we are lucky enough to see a grizzly bear den close up. This den is a typical one—located at the base of a big old cedar tree, on a steep mountainside about 600 metres above sea level, with a southern exposure. The sides of the den entrance are polished smooth as varnished wood. Caught on the tree bark are hairs of a light-coloured grizzly bear, and in the inner cavern we find hairs of other colours and shades, evidence of generations of bears using this retreat to sleep away the cold, wet winters. The small scratches in the den cavity were probably inflicted by a restless cub eager to see if there was more to life than the inside of this tree. Porcupine quills lie on the floor, probably having been dislodged last winter from some resident's snout. Thick layers of feathery moss have been brought in to cover the floor, a soft cushion for the long sleep. We spend so much time observing territory, sedges, salmon—everything a bear requires when it is awake—we had long overlooked the habitat where it spends the other half of its life. It is as if we have finally seen the biggest missing piece of the bear's life cycle.

About 18 kilometres north of Green Inlet on Princess Royal Channel is the steep-sided, 8-kilometre-long Khutze Inlet, and at the head of the inlet is the mouth of the Khutze River. Waterfalls cascading down from all sides make this one of the more picturesque spots on the coast. In the 1920s and '30s, a mine operated here with an aerial tram and a railway that ran between the camp and the mine site. Small-scale logging operations came and went, and although most of the inlet forest is logged, the more remote river valley remains unscathed. Today helicopters fly in and out, assessing new logging and mining possibilities.

Ian inspects recent grizzly bear diggings in the estuary.

OPPOSITE **The pride of the Khutze is its estuary, a wide expanse of angelica, sedges and numerous other plants that make up a major part of a grizzly bear's diet.**

KAREN'S JOURNAL : I figure that if a 500-pound grizzly can make do on a bunch of grasses and sedges and tubers, I ought to be able to gather enough for one dinner for Ian and me. Armed with a trowel and bucket, I set out to live off the fat of the land. I dig up a few bulbs of the rice root, a member of the lily family so named because the bulbs look like tightly wrapped bundles of rice. Next I gather leaves of Sitka burnet, mint and a few aster flowers. At the edge of the flats I find dessert—giant orange salmonberries and red huckleberries, with a few gooseberries tossed in for good measure. I walk along the edge of the river picking leaves from the odd willowherb and brooklime, snag a few monkey-flowers, and come across a small patch of miner's lettuce. Looking down, I can't help noticing that my bucket is not even half full, and I have been out here for a long, long time. Hats off to the grizzly.

The pride of the Khutze is its estuary, a wide expanse of angelica, sedges and numerous other plants that make up a major part of a grizzly bear's diet. Lyngby's sedge, which is almost 25 percent crude protein in its early growth stages, is a favourite. Bears make use of a wide diversity of plants and eat different parts of the same plant throughout its growing season. The BC government's 1993 Khutzeymateen Valley Grizzly Bear Study documented grizzly bear use of over fifty plants, from the emerging leaf buds of devil's club in early spring to the energy-packed corms and roots of angelica and lovage in the late fall. When we approach the estuary in the spring, the first thing we see are the great holes left by grizzly bears digging up plant roots. The bears act as nature's rototillers. They also help propagate berries and flowering plants by dispersing seeds in their scat.

The Aaltanhash Inlet, with the pristine Aaltanhash River at its head, is neighbour to the Khutze on the north, just across Princess Royal Channel from the disused cannery and fish packing centre of Butedale. When we pull in about midday, two Sitka deer stand unmoving in the estuary, watching our approach. The last time we were here it was pouring rain and the desire to explore was less ardent. Now the sun is shining, there's not a cloud in the sky, and the horizon with its not-so-far-away mountains is most enticing.

IAN'S JOURNAL : We take the canoe up to the head of the Aaltanhash, then we hike up until we reach a stand of enormous spruce trees alongside a vast meadow. Karen climbs one of the trees for a look and a big grin beaming down at me tells me she has spotted something. I scramble up a neighbouring tree and there, standing well above the hardhack, is the very large headset of a moose, the first I've ever seen on the coast. He is a young bull, but stands at least 2 metres off the ground with his antlers. Nostrils the size of pancakes work in and out as he strains to make out some scent that is not quite right—us, I assume. But then a loud skirmish comes from a tree on the opposite side of the meadow and down slides a great big black bear. It all makes sense when I spot a grizzly walking away on the other side of the meadow. Clearly the grizzly has chased the black bear up the tree and kept him there until we came along. By the time Karen and I head back, we are tired from a long, full day. We hike back to where we left the canoe, and as we drift down the slow waters of the Aaltanhash in the fading light, the memories of all we have seen today are still vivid in our minds. And still the day is not quite over. A varied thrush pierces the silence with its raspy whistle, and a beaver slaps its tail down hard before somersaulting underwater. Up ahead a wolf sits unmoving, watching us as we glide by in the canoe. We stop paddling in mid-stroke, and for a few moments, nothing can be heard but drops of water falling from the tips of the blades. We drift past the wolf, staring into his eyes, until the Aaltanhash carries us from view. This evening and this valley could not be more divine, more primeval, more wild.

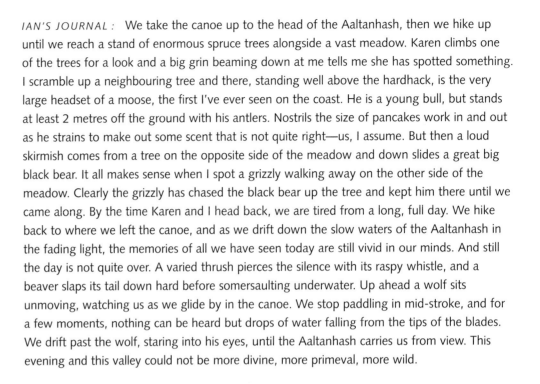

BELOW AND OPPOSITE **On a perfect day of hiking and canoeing in the Aaltanhash River valley, Karen and Ian encounter a solitary wolf, a beaver and a display of Indian paintbrush in full bloom.**

The deep inland fiords of Douglas Channel and Gardner Canal define the territories of the Haisla nation, whose traditional lands also include five eulachon-bearing rivers—the Kitlope, Kowesas, Kemano, Kildala and Kitimat. Of these, only the Kitlope and Kowesas still have intact rainforest. The Kildala and Kitimat have been badly damaged, and the grease-making camps have been abandoned. Travelling up the Gardner Canal for the first time is an experience that no one can be prepared for—130 kilometres of sheer granite walls rising from water tinted jade green by glacial runoff. Hundreds of mountain goats line the upper reaches of the rock walls. But the Gardner Canal has a long history of logging. Its banks have been stripped clean to supply mills in Kitimat and Vancouver, and the gutted landscapes around the lower reaches—at Crab Lake, Sleeman Creek, Kiltuish Inlet and Pike Creek, for instance—are not a pretty sight.

By the early 1990s, logging plans were also in the works for the scattered lower-elevation rainforests of the mountainous Kitlope River valley, about 30 kilometres east of Fiordland. But the Haisla and Henaaksiala and a coalition of environmental groups worked

Mountain goats can be sighted in most raincoast inlets with steep shores, and they appear by the hundreds in the Gardner Canal. In the winter months goats often come down to tidewater, where Ian and Karen have watched them feed on seaweed.

LEFT The pristine Brim River flows into the Gardner Canal at Owyacumish Bay.

OPPOSITE Looking into Owyacumish Bay on Gardner Canal. All who follow the Gardner Canal deep into the traditional territories of the Haisla and Henaaksiala find the opalescent green of its glacier-fed waters an unforgettable sight.

long and hard to secure full protection of the area, which local First Nations identify as a "power spot." Since 1994 the 317,000-hectare Kitlope Heritage Conservancy Protected Area (Huchsduwachsdu Nuyem Jees) has been managed jointly by the provincial government and the Haisla people. The Haisla and an environmental group called Ecotrust have begun work to protect the Kowesas watershed, about one-tenth the size of the Kitlope and like a miniature version of it. But for the Kitimat River, at the head of Douglas Channel, it is too late.

Haisla refers to people who live at the mouth of the river. The roads that lead here from the northeast and northwest follow ancient grease trails—trade routes named after their main commodity, eulachon grease—and the First Nations village of Kitamaat is located here. But so is Kitimat, an industrial town built in the 1950s around the Aluminum Company of Canada's (Alcan) smelter and a large pulp mill.

To get there, we sail up to Kitimat Arm through Devastation Channel—whose name, which came from a British ship, has an ironic resonance today.

In Kitamaat Village we buy a salmon dinner at a food stand on the edge of the soccer field. (In New York City, there are hot dog and pretzel stands; in Kitamaat, sockeye salmon stands.) At the edge of town is a small cabin with a sign that says: "Arts and Crafts." It turns out to be the workshop of Haisla carver Sammy Robinson, where many of his fine carvings are on display. We admire a silver pendant with a grizzly bear carved on it, and Sammy tells us he grew up in a river valley full of grizzly bears, the Giltoyees River valley about halfway down Douglas Channel. But he warns us that we won't find many grizzlies there today.

When we leave Kitimat, we sail into the Giltoyees Inlet, a popular recreation area for people in the area. There we see a black bear wandering through the middle of the estuary without a care in the world. Grizzly bears rarely tolerate black bears in prime habitat like estuaries—they push them into less productive habitat farther from the river. So when you see a black bear where you should be seeing a grizzly, you know something is wrong.

The estuary is intact, there's salmon in the rivers, and there are trees all around. But we notice a distinct scarcity of wildlife here, and when we flip through the guestbook at the hunting and fishing cabin in the bay, we see that we are not the first visitors to notice it. We can only conclude that most of the grizzly bears in the Giltoyees have been shot.

Tracks like these were becoming increasingly rare in the Kitlope River valley until the Haisla nation was successful in having a moratorium placed on trophy hunting of grizzlies in the area.

OPPOSITE This family of tagged grizzlies was moved into the Kowesas River valley on Gardner Canal from the nearby community of Kemano. The Haisla nation is working to protect the pristine Kowesas in conjunction with the Kitlope.

OPPOSITE The 317,000-hectare Kitlope Valley was granted protection in 1994, following a concerted campaign by the Haisla people and a coalition of conservation groups.

Speaking of the Kitimat River, Henaaksiala Chief Cecil Paul says, "I have seen a lot of changes in my life. I saw my grandfather take down a deer with a bow and arrow and I saw a man put a foot on the moon. But if you told me in my lifetime I would witness the death of a great river, I would never have believed it."

That's what happened in the neighbouring Foch River valley, and in the Kitlope at the head of Gardner Canal. In the Kitlope, the Haisla managed to get a moratorium on grizzly bear hunting in the hope that the population would recover. "The Kitlope is like the bank of our people," says Henaaksiala Hereditary Chief Cecil Paul. "We have always only touched upon its interest, whether it be salmon or eulachon, crabapple or berries. We never touched the capital. This financial agreement made us a very wealthy people for thousands of years."

CHAPTER FOUR

NORTH *to the* BORDER

The northern raincoast, from Douglas Channel to the Kshwan River at the head of Hastings Arm, is an environment of contradictions. One moment you can stand in a valley in the wildest region on the coast, the next moment you're downwind of a huge mill. Kitimat, at the head of Douglas Channel, is dominated by its aluminum smelter and pulp mill, and Prince Rupert is a seaport city of 16,000 people with its own pulp mill. But despite the proximity of well-established human populations, many of the valleys in this area remain largely

Nootka lupines present a symphony of colour in the estuary of the Kshwan River, in Hastings Arm at the northern extreme of the Great Bear Rainforest.

ALASKA

USA

Portland Canal

Hastings Arm

Anyox

Alice Arm

Kshwan Ck.

Ohl Ck.

Stagoo Ck.

Observatory Inlet

Nass River

Kincolith

Greenville

Nass Bay

Burton Ck.

Johnson Ck.

Chambers Ck.

Kwinamass R.

Portland Inlet

Khutzeymateen R.

Chatham Sound

Lax Kw'alaams

Work Channel

Khyex R.

Exchamsiks R.

Skeena River

Metlakatla

Prince Rupert

Inverness Passage

KAIEN ISLAND

Skeena River

Gitnadoix R.

Kitimat River

Port Essington

Khtada Lake

Kitimat

Brown Lake

Kitamaat Village

Jesse L.

PORCHER ISLAND

Telegraph Passage

Festall R.

Gitloyees Inlet

Dala River

Foch R.

Kildala R.

Hecate Strait

PITT ISLAND

Grenville Channel

Lowe Inlet

Kitkiata Inlet

Douglas Channel

HAWKESBURY ISLAND

Sleeman Ck.

Devastation Channel

Crab Lake

Brim R.

BANKS ISLAND

Principe Channel

Hartley Bay

GRIBBELL ISL.

Gardner Canal

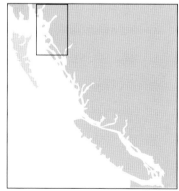

0   25   50 kilometres

0   10   20   30 miles

unspoiled. This northern section of the Great Bear Rainforest encompasses a string of wilderness watersheds that run all the way to the Alaska border. Of the thirty remaining intact watersheds in this region, only two of them, the Khutzeymateen and the Gitnadoix, are protected.

Sailing out of Douglas Channel after leaving Kitimat, we enter the traditional lands of the Coast Tsimshian, whose cultural heartland is still the lower region of the salmon-rich, fast-flowing Skeena River, but whose ancestral territory extends from Princess Royal Island to the Portland Canal. Farther east, about 20 kilometres from the mouth of Douglas Channel, we turn into Kitkiata Inlet. At its head is the Quaal River valley, which

Shoreline petroglyphs on Douglas Channel are vivid reminders of days not so long ago when First Nations peoples had this territory all to themselves.

Karen cautiously approaches a young grizzly too absorbed in his salmon fishing to pay her much attention. The McAllisters try to walk the fine line of observing bears without interfering in their daily pursuits.

OPPOSITE The height of land between the 21,000-hectare Quaal River valley and the larger Ecstall valley to the north is so low that the two systems form one continuous rainforest region of more than 100,000 hectares.

used to be the southern terminus of a well-travelled grease trail that runs north to the Ecstall River, a large tributary of the Skeena. Together the Quaal and Ecstall valleys form one continuous rainforest region of over 100,000 hectares. The two rivers are only shouting distance apart, and the land between them is just high enough to send their waters flowing in opposite directions. We haven't had any luck finding grizzlies in the Quaal, but Fisheries patroller Stan Hutchings tells us he saw a grizzly there last summer, and we are glad to hear it. Stan has spent most of his career slogging along the creeks and rivers of the Great Bear coast, and when we ask him how many grizzlies he has encountered over the years, he thinks for a moment before answering, "Hundreds." He once shot at a grizzly bear in self-defence, but now he thinks he may have been too quick to pull the trigger. It has been years since he carried a gun in the forest. We pay close attention to reports of violent encounters between people and grizzlies, but find most of them occur away from the coast and often involve bears that are human habituated, i.e. they have learned to associate people with food and guns. Some people like Stan, who know both areas, feel coastal grizzlies are less aggressive than their interior relations, no doubt partly because the coast bears' bellies are full of salmon for such a large part of their active season. Our own experience certainly supports this, but we still try to be cautious and mostly stay out of their way. We always travel with a good supply of bear-repellent pepper spray, but are guided by the words of bear attack expert Stephen Herrero that the best weapon to use when travelling in bear country is your brain.

KAREN'S JOURNAL : As we swerve around the shallow oxbow curves of the Quaal River, hundreds of eagles glide above us and the bay is full of chubby little seals—a sure sign that the salmon have arrived. It is a hot day, and we seek refuge in the shade of the spruces that line the Quaal. The water squirms with chum and pink salmon, most of which have already turned a queasy colour of green and red. The stench of rotting fish is overpowering. These salmon elders seem to be withering before my eyes, but through the rippled surface of the water I can see their sparkling legacy on the gravel bottom. A smattering of tiny eggs lies uncovered, twinkling like pink stars under the glare of the sunlight.

At the headwaters of the Quaal, we are just a skip from the Ecstall River, but to reach it by water we sail back down Douglas Channel, past the small Native community of

Hartley Bay, and point northwest into Grenville Channel toward the mouth of the Skeena. On our way, we make a detour to Campania Island on the outer coast. We find Campania to be mostly bog with the odd gnarled shore pine—not the best place for a larger mammal to live. The most dangerous predator seems to be a tiny plant called sundew. Covered with distinctive reddish hairs and topped by a glandular dewdrop, the sundew obtains its quota of nitrogen by trapping and devouring the insects that are attracted to it. Even in this bleak terrain there are sheltered ravines full of colourful mosses and small creeks, some of which produce salmon. It is easy to tell the ones with salmon runs by the added richness of the moss and lichens on their banks, the legacy of thousands of years of good fish fertilizer. We can only dart out for short periods of time because the rain is coming down with such force we have to shout to be heard under the shelter of the *Companion's* deck. Finally, on the third day, we find ourselves longing to see the sun set. It is months since we witnessed the sun actually making it all the way to the horizon. We decide to head back up Grenville Channel toward the Skeena, and it proves to be a good move—the weather clears up immediately.

Grenville Channel, locally nicknamed Granville Street in honour of Vancouver's main downtown thoroughfare, is a straight 80-kilometre alley of water running between Pitt Island and the mainland. BC Ferries calls it the Grand Canyon of the coast but a boat our

OPPOSITE **Streaking toward its target like a combat fighter plane, the rare Peale's peregrine falcon feeds on live birds taken on the wing. Seabirds such as auklets are favourite prey.**

BELOW LEFT **Typical of the outer coastal islands, the windswept and treeless Campania Island is part of a rugged archipelago that shields the rainforest valleys of the mainland from the worst of the Pacific storms.**

BELOW RIGHT **Western sandpiper.**

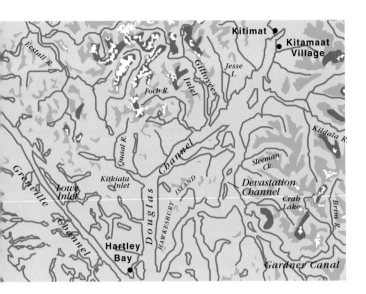

size that only travels at about 6 knots under power is generally out of luck here when the wind and tide join forces against it. On this trip, a high pressure zone has firmly fixed itself on the coast, bringing the first stretch of real summer weather we have felt this year. The skies are clear and for once the boat gets thoroughly dry inside and out. But you can't win, it seems—this relief from wetness also brings long days of gale-force westerlies that turn Grenville into a wind tunnel and force even the tugs and fish boats to seek refuge in the protected waters of Lowe Inlet, about 25 kilometres up the channel.

KAREN'S JOURNAL : While Ian hikes up to one of the clearcuts overlooking Lowe Inlet, I paddle to the falls for a more pleasant view. All around me fish are jumping, their bodies catapulting out of the water and fins skimming the surface like miniature porpoises. Occasionally a salmon attempts to fling itself up the cataract. Last night, when Ian was standing by the side of the waterfall with his camera poised, a flying salmon hit him so hard on the chin it left a bruise that will probably last all week.

Many prominent sites along the northern coast, like this area above scenic Lowe Inlet, are privately owned and can be logged without regulation.

118

Bald eagles congregate in high numbers when salmon return to their home rivers to spawn.

Salmon perform some truly remarkable feats ascending falls and rapids to reach their spawning grounds. These airborne coho attempt to navigate a falls in Verney River, Lowe Inlet.

FOLLOWING PAGES The breathtaking Foch River valley empties into Douglas Channel 40 kilometres from Kitimat.

ABOVE **Up the Skeena River, past the Khtada River, is the Gitnadoix Recreation Area, a spectacular 56,800-hectare river system characterized by large areas of wetland, but little productive rainforest.**

RIGHT **The Skeena River supports the second largest commercial fishery in BC, second only to the Fraser.**

OPPOSITE **The 84,000-hectare Ecstall River system is the largest intact unprotected watershed in coastal BC. It supports five species of salmon and has uncommonly large tracts of prized Sitka spruce.**

Grenville Channel opens into Telegraph Passage at its north end. We bear right and sail into the mighty Skeena, second only to the Fraser among BC rivers, with a broad 580-kilometre main stem and over a hundred tributaries probing far into the BC interior. Only its lower reaches can be described as true rainforest country, and just two of the rainforest river valleys on the north side of the river, the Exchamsiks and the Khyex, remain intact. Both rivers wind their way between steep cliffs, through breathtaking landscape. On the south side, lovely Khtada Lake at the head of Khtada River remains pristine, but is threatened by logging.

The sun is almost setting by the time we drop the hook near the mouth of the Ecstall River, about 10 kilometres upriver. Beneath a black sky, a string of more than forty lights from fishing boats glint from the western shore of the Skeena. The gillnetters are out on a twenty-four-hour sockeye opening. With its shallow bars and strong currents the river can do terrible things to nets, but the Skeena sockeye run, BC's second largest, has been one of the few bright spots in recent fishing seasons. Our radio crackles with a message from Fisheries patroller Dave Lewis. "Shoulda known it was you! Who else would come so far up the Skeena on a falling tide—and in the middle of an opening!"

The rollicking cannery town of Port Essington once stood here, on the muddy banks where the Ecstall meets the Skeena.

The Ecstall survives as the largest intact unprotected rainforest valley in Canada. To us, it is the most ecologically diverse and fascinating wild rainforest on the coast. Sailing up this river is the closest we can come to experiencing what one of the major rivers like the Fraser or the Nass must have looked like before the arrival of the Europeans. Unlike most raincoast rivers, the Ecstall is wide, shallow and filled with mucky silt. When we take the Zodiac up a side channel, we find a tangle of streamside vegetation overhanging the gooey, narrow banks. The muddy water turns crystal clear, revealing a stream bottom layered in soft brown gravel. This is just the way the salmon like it, and coho and chum are known to swim 100 kilometres up the Ecstall and its tributaries to spawn.

BELOW Now in total ruin, Port Essington at the confluence of the Ecstall and Skeena rivers was once a booming commercial centre with several canneries. A colourful piece of coastal history disappears as rainforest growth reclaims the old Port Essington cemetery. A child identified only as Emily was three when she was laid to rest here in 1890.

Robust growth of skunk cabbage and strong salmon runs make the Ecstall River valley prime grizzly bear habitat.

ABOVE Asters grow wild on the north coast.

RIGHT The wide floodplain of the Ecstall valley supports one of the most extensive intact Sitka spruce forests remaining on the northwest coast. Old-growth spruce like this multi-headed giant are much sought after by loggers for their strong, light wood, but play an irreplaceable role in the rainforest ecosystem.

KAREN'S JOURNAL : It never ceases to amaze me how water can travel from the tip of a tree root 75 metres to the top of a tree, in a magical feat called "cohesion." One little water molecule at the top of the water column attracting another little water molecule, and so on, and so on.

What happens underground is even more amazing. To draw water and other nutrients from the ground, trees need the help of fungi that attach themselves to the roots. These fungi send out long, threadlike fibres that interweave and attach to other roots, creating a massive underground network that links together the smallest mushroom and the tallest Sitka spruce. The fungi in turn need the nutrients that the tree can provide. The soil on the floor of an old-growth forest contains some 4.5 tonnes of life-giving fungal strands per hectare. Under my feet is a living, growing entity that runs deep into the earth.

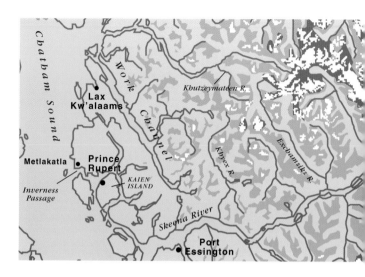

The broad tract of undisturbed forest between the Ecstall and the Quaal makes for very diverse wildlife. It is the only place we have found wolverine tracks fresh enough to follow, though we had to admit defeat when the trail disappeared into the rising tide. The presence of wolverine may be a better indicator than even grizzly bears that the wilderness environment is all there. Wolverine have extremely far-reaching ranges—they can be feeding on a mountain goat carcass in the icefields one day and dragging salmon from a valley bottom the next.

To reach Prince Rupert, on the western edge of Kaien Island, we catch the ebbing tide

A rare sight on the raincoast, osprey prefer to nest on freshwater lakes.

With a population of 16,500, the deep-sea port of Prince Rupert is the largest city in the Great Bear Rainforest area.

OPPOSITE One of the most awesome of the many industrial ruins found throughout the the northern BC coast is this abandoned copper smelter at the ghost town of Anyox on Observatory Inlet.

and sail back down the Skeena heading northwest through Inverness Passage. This part of the coast was once richly populated with Tsimshian winter villages, and the Skeena was dotted with summer fishing communities. The largest centre on the north coast, Prince Rupert has the shallowest historical roots, having been started in 1906 by developers of the Grand Trunk Pacific Railway, who hoped it would soon overtake Vancouver as western Canada's leading port. It fell a good deal short on that score, but it is still the cultural and economic heart of the north coast.

Just across the bay from Prince Rupert, the picturesque First Nations village of Metlakatla was originally the principal winter gathering place of the main Coast Tsimshian tribes. About 30 kilometres farther north is the Coast Tsimshian community of Lax Kw'alaams (Port Simpson), one of the coast's largest First Nations settlements. A few kilometres past Lax Kw'alaams we round Father Point into the waters of BC's longest and most northerly inlet complex, the Portland Inlet – Portland Canal – Observatory Inlet system, which marks the border between BC and Alaska. In the late evening we reach the Khutzeymateen Inlet, home of BC's only grizzly bear preserve, but we decide to bypass it until our return. We spend the night a few kilometres north at the mouth of the Kwinamass River. In the morning, exploring its broad and sedge-filled estuary, we find that a grizzly has been churning up the leaf stems of some late-season skunk cabbage. Its paw prints are everywhere.

We continue northeast and stop in Nass Bay, about 45 kilometres up Portland Inlet. Some twenty creeks and rivers, including the Nass River, empty into this beautiful bay. Three large watersheds here—Burton, Chambers and Johnson creeks—remain unroaded, although activity has recently begun in the Chambers and the Johnson is slated to be next. All three are salmon rivers which form part of the traditional territory of the Nisga'a, the people of the Nass. The annual eulachon run up the Nass lies at the core of Nisga'a mythology, and about 2,500 Nisga'a live in the rugged landscape that surrounds the Nass all along its 380-kilometre length. The Nisga'a are in the process of negotiating a comprehensive land claims agreement with the provincial and federal governments, and development plans for Burton Creek are on hold until the Nisga'a agreement is signed. Unfortunately, much more logging could be under way soon, regardless of the nature of the final agreement.

Portland Inlet takes us to Observatory Inlet, which carries us north to Hastings Arm, and at the head of this waterway lies the Kshwan River. Nestled under the Cambria Icefield more than 200 kilometres north of Prince Rupert, the Kshwan is the northern-most intact river valley in the Great Bear Rainforest area. It is ominous and lonely along

this stretch, yet it feels wild and good. On the way up Hastings Arm to the Kshwan River the sides of the fiord are so steep a tree has no hope of clinging to them. Huge waterfalls tumble from above. The Kshwan itself is a wild river flowing a glacial grey-green. In its lower regions it is a huge, shifting waterway that meanders through extensive cottonwood forests in a flat-bottomed valley. Farther up, salmon spawn in the tiniest trickles right along the tongues of the icefields. Here, great hotel-sized blocks of granite lie strewn along the water's edge. In the wide open wetlands, in sand formed from eroded granite, grizzly bears have fashioned their daybeds—dish-shaped hollows about a metre long, a metre wide and 30 centimetres deep in which they nap for a few hours at a time during the day or night.

At the mouth of the Kshwan River we are at the very edge of the raincoast, on the fringe of the interior boreal forest. Here, intricate bear trails wind around conifers that are etched with deep black scars left by bear claws. The trees, which are oozing white sap, have been rubbed shiny by generations of grizzly bears removing their shedding coats. Never have we seen so many elaborate rubbing trees in one valley, or so many succulent green sedges. The entire Kshwan region is rich in bear food and laced with bear trails—it is a grizzly bear playground. Yet we don't actually see any bears. The explanation may be in reports we've had of people cruising the river in jet boats, firing indiscriminately at the bears on shore. In one place we find a grizzly skull that has been placed on a branch about 3 metres up a tree.

Karen inspects a tree in the Kshwan River valley marked by grizzly bears. These so-called "mark trees" are not wholly understood but may serve as a kind of rainforest registry, defining territory and allowing bears to announce their presence to each other.

IAN'S JOURNAL : Can't seem to stop. I've been at it all day, each bend in the river drawing me on like a spawning salmon. I started out early this morning under the coolness of a late summer fog but by around eleven the sun burst through and has kept the temperature high until now. The long shadows falling onto the muddy waters should have told me to turn back some time ago—but what is around the next bend? I remember asking Stan Hutchings what keeps him wandering up these raincoast rivers. He is contracted by the Department of Fisheries, but his work has long since materialized into something more. That "something more" is what keeps Karen and me coming back.

The Khutzeymateen River sits like a miracle at the end of Khutzeymateen Inlet. Like the Gardner Canal, this inlet has seen its share of logging, but the river valley itself is essentially pristine. Exceptional stands of Sitka spruce trees line the valley bottom, and four species of salmon spawn in the river, inspiring a congregation of seals and sea lions and even an occasional humpback whale to hang around the river mouth.

In 1994 Prince Philip flew into the Khutzeymateen to help inaugurate the establishment

OPPOSITE An adult male grizzly in the valley of the Kwinamass River, next to the Khutzeymateen. Bears frequently wander from the protected confines of the Khutzeymateen to surrounding valleys where they are fair game for hunters.

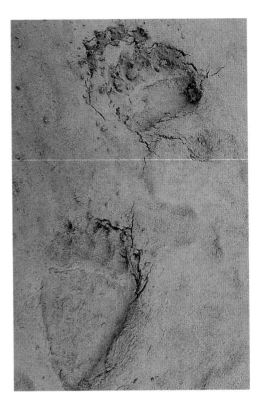

Grizzly bear tracks.

OPPOSITE **Protecting the remaining intact rainforest systems that range between Knight Inlet to the south and the Kshwan River to the north is the only way to protect the coastal grizzly bear and its globally unique temperate rainforest habitat.**

of a 45,000-hectare provincial park and grizzly bear sanctuary. The Khutzeymateen is believed to be the home of fifty to sixty bears—the highest known concentration of grizzlies on the entire coast. The park is now jointly managed by the BC government and the Tsimshian Nation, expressly for the protection of the bears. Only authorized guides are allowed on the river and visitors are not permitted ashore. The bears have become partially accustomed to the presence of humans, and studies done at the McNeil River State Game Sanctuary in Alaska show that where bears are habituated to neither guns nor food, they are able to coexist peacefully with people in a guardedly neutral relationship.

Visiting the Khutzeymateen always leaves us with powerfully mixed emotions. The success of the two-decade-long campaign by environmentalists that led to protection of the Khutzeymateen is an inspiration and a source of hope to all who care about the coastal grizzly and the rainforest habitat of the northern coast. On the other hand, it is frustrating to see the Khutzeymateen used over and over again to reassure the public that the BC government's grizzly management policies are sound, and that the grizzly problem has somehow been taken care of. The area provides protection for only about 2.5 percent of the coast's grizzlies, and the safety of even those few is anything but guaranteed. A study of radio-collared Khutzeymateen grizzlies, conducted by the BC Ministry of Environment, Lands and Parks between 1989 and 1993, found that the bears often cross the high ridges from the sanctuary into other watersheds, and when this happens they become fair game for hunters. This is why setting aside small areas cannot protect a species like the grizzly bear: their range is measured not in one river valley but in clusters of river valleys that may cover hundreds of thousands of hectares, and they don't stay within park boundaries.

The Khutzeymateen represents one small but significant step toward safeguarding the raincoast wilderness. But the protection of the coastal grizzly and all the other life forms of the rainforest will not be complete until more areas are reserved to form one large, integrated wild environment. The alternative is a largely industrialized landscape surrounding several isolated islands of ancient forest and one bear sanctuary. This is far from being a workable blueprint for safeguarding biological diversity and protecting some of the earth's most precious wilderness.

THE GREAT BEAR RAINFOREST
PROPOSAL

The decision to produce a book about the Great Bear Rainforest was not an easy one to make, partly because one book can barely do justice to even one individual river valley, but also because it feels like we are somehow betraying the secrets of a private and mysterious world. The responsibility of putting words in the place of things that should be felt, and photographs in place of true experience, weighs on us, as does the responsibility for doing justice to the First Nations people who have been worthy stewards of the raincoast for thousands of years.

But this magnificent natural heritage is disappearing before our eyes. We can count fifteen large rainforest valleys that have been opened up to logging between 1990 and 1997, and at the time of writing forty more were scheduled to fall. After the remaining valleys are gone, there will be no others. That is the defining fact—not only are these pristine valleys facing their last days, they are the last of their kind in all creation. Knowing that, we felt we must make this attempt to show what we have found, and to propose a way to save it.

We advocate protection of the remaining intact rainforest watersheds along the northern BC coast. This is what has become known as the Great Bear Rainforest Proposal. Each individual valley is precious and rare, and together they represent our final hope of protecting a fully functioning ecosystem large enough to ensure the survival of the ancient temperate rainforest, the coastal grizzly bear, hundreds of stocks of wild salmon and the thousands of other species that depend on old-growth forest. This is a proposal in principle. Implementation would require creative approaches like those used in Alaska and in the Clayoquot region of BC, or perhaps something different. Detailed strategies remain to be worked out in an inclusive and democratic process.

We make this proposal with humility and awareness of its considerable implications. We know how extreme it may appear, calling as it does for some form of protection over a greater land mass than any park or reserve currently existing in British Columbia. But we feel there are two extenuating circumstances that make our proposal not just reasonable but necessary at this time.

First, this area is comprised mostly of rock, ice and scrub forest. The fertile portion where the salmon, bears and merchantable timber are found makes up less than 7 percent of the entire area enclosed within the Great Bear Proposal, or about 224,000 hectares out of the 3.2-million-hectare total. There are many precedents for protected areas of this size, especially in areas of world heritage significance.

Second and much more important, this is the last chance. To the south, everything that can be logged either has been logged or soon will be. If the northern BC coast is logged too, humankind will have obliterated one of nature's most impressive biological regimes from the face of the earth, except for a few isolated patches which are not large enough to sustain themselves. This makes the situation today entirely different from the one facing earlier generations, to whom old-growth forests seemed to go on forever. They did not go on forever, and we are now looking at the last sustainable piece. This is a fundamentally different situation than North Americans have ever faced before and it calls for a fundamentally different response. It does not indicate business as usual.

Unfortunately, business as usual is exactly what government and industry have offered in their initial responses to the Great Bear Proposal. Most of the arguments they make are familiar ones, but there are special raincoast twists.

GOVERNMENT AND INDUSTRY POINT TO THE many outstanding parks created in the Khutzeymateen and Kitlope river valleys, and the Gitnadoix, Fiordland and Hakai recreation areas, and say 10.7 percent

Clearcut to both stream banks, this rainforest watershed on Gilford Island has been destroyed for generations to come. Devastation like this continues to be permitted on the coast despite government claims the 1995 Forest Practices Code gave British Columbia the strictest logging regulations in the world.

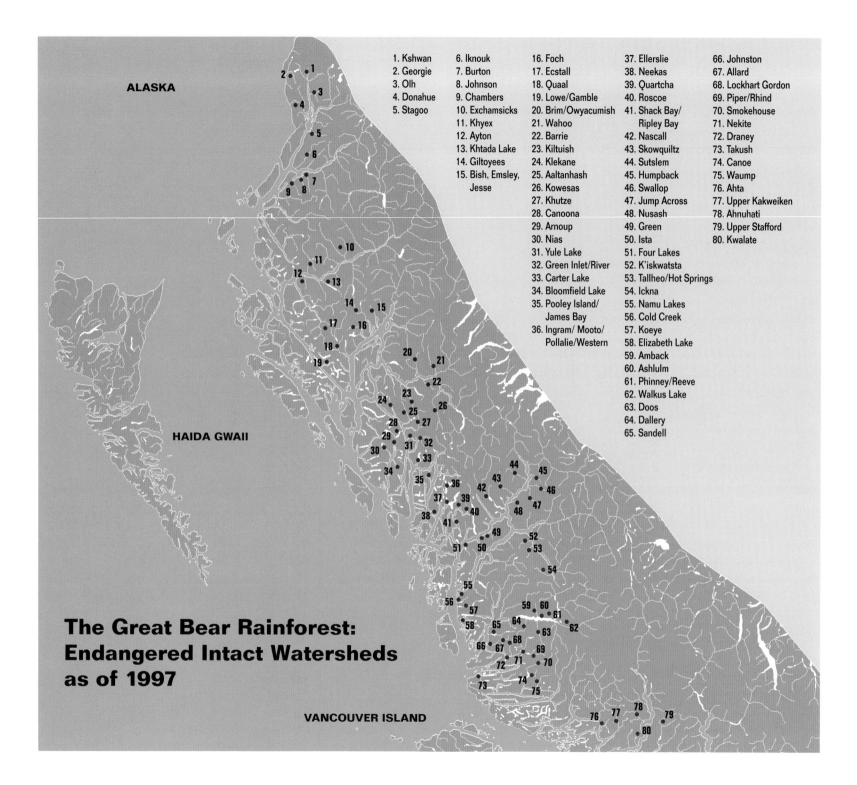

ALASKA

1. Kshwan
2. Georgie
3. Olh
4. Donahue
5. Stagoo
6. Iknouk
7. Burton
8. Johnson
9. Chambers
10. Exchamsicks
11. Khyex
12. Ayton
13. Khtada Lake
14. Giltoyees
15. Bish, Emsley, Jesse
16. Foch
17. Ecstall
18. Quaal
19. Lowe/Gamble
20. Brim/Owyacumish
21. Wahoo
22. Barrie
23. Kiltuish
24. Klekane
25. Aaltanhash
26. Kowesas
27. Khutze
28. Canoona
29. Arnoup
30. Nias
31. Yule Lake
32. Green Inlet/River
33. Carter Lake
34. Bloomfield Lake
35. Pooley Island/ James Bay
36. Ingram/ Mooto/ Pollalie/Western
37. Ellerslie
38. Neekas
39. Quartcha
40. Roscoe
41. Shack Bay/ Ripley Bay
42. Nascall
43. Skowquiltz
44. Sutslem
45. Humpback
46. Swallop
47. Jump Across
48. Nusash
49. Green
50. Ista
51. Four Lakes
52. K'iskwatsta
53. Tallheo/Hot Springs
54. Ickna
55. Namu Lakes
56. Cold Creek
57. Koeye
58. Elizabeth Lake
59. Amback
60. Ashlulm
61. Phinney/Reeve
62. Walkus Lake
63. Doos
64. Dallery
65. Sandell
66. Johnston
67. Allard
68. Lockhart Gordon
69. Piper/Rhind
70. Smokehouse
71. Nekite
72. Draney
73. Takush
74. Canoe
75. Waump
76. Ahta
77. Upper Kakweiken
78. Ahnuhati
79. Upper Stafford
80. Kwalate

HAIDA GWAII

The Great Bear Rainforest: Endangered Intact Watersheds as of 1997

VANCOUVER ISLAND

of the central coast land base has already been protected, which is close enough to its province-wide target of 12 percent to rule out new large-scale park creation. Environmental groups have responded by pointing out that, scenic as much of it is, the areas set aside on the northern coast are predominantly rock, ice and scrub forest containing a low percentage of productive rainforest, and therefore incapable of protecting the full spectrum of rainforest species from extinction. In conservation terms it is as if Brazil agreed to preserve 12 percent of its wilderness, then set aside a few million hectares of mountain peaks while stepping up the job of liquidating its rainforest.

When protecting 12 percent of the earth's natural areas first became established as a global target following the 1987 United Nations World Commission on Environment and Development (a.k.a. the Brundtland Commission), its proponents made clear that 12 percent was a minimum, not a maximum, and that it was a short-term goal to be achieved by the year 2000. It was never intended that

the effort to preserve natural habitat should stop there, and leading conservation biologists like Michael Soulé have warned that stopping at 12 percent could push half the world's species over the brink into extinction. Further, it was clearly understood that if protecting 12 percent of natural habitat was to have any effect in preserving global biodiversity, each representative ecosystem had to be protected, not just the unproductive areas with little commercial value. This goal of protecting viable examples of natural ecosystems was adopted by the BC Protected Areas Strategy when it was initiated in 1992. On the BC coast this would have meant protecting 12 percent or 840,000 hectares of BC's total temperate rainforest area of 7 million hectares, but with only 408,000 hectares protected to date, that goal has not been even halfway reached. Protecting the roughly estimated 224,000 hectares of productive forest in the Great Bear Proposal represents the only real

opportunity for bringing BC close to the goal of saving 12 percent of its temperate rainforest, but even then it would fall short, as the amount of protected rainforest in the province would increase to just slightly more than 9 percent.

THE FOREST INDUSTRY CLAIMS clearcut logging does not destroy the rainforest, but only renews it the same way nature renews it. They say that the present forest on the northern BC coast is overmature and can be made more productive by clearing it off and replacing it with even-aged tree plantations. This is what the forest industry is doing virtually everywhere else in the Pacific Northwest, and whether or not it will work the way they say remains a very big question mark. But two points are clear. First, the young, managed forests loggers leave behind are not the same as the old, wild forests they take away. The eminent US Forest Service ecologist Jerry Franklin put it simply: "Old growth differs markedly from a forest managed by humans. Its ecosystem takes two to three hundred years to develop along the Northwest's wet coastal strip." And even after 300 years, the forest only begins to acquire characteristics the original forest developed over thousands of years. The young plantation forests are designed to be reharvested every 100–150 years, meaning the old-growth ecosystem will never have a chance to rebuild. Second, nobody is denying industrial loggers the opportunity to convert the vast bulk of the ancient temperate rainforest into timber plantations. That is already well under way, and if they cannot make their grand experiment work with the huge territory already under development, the northern coast's small contribution will not make any difference. But it is one thing to convert most of the rainforest into a fibre factory, and quite another thing to convert every last bit of it. As the noted forest zoologist Chris Maser has written, "To lose old-growth forests is to cast ourselves adrift in a sea of

ABOVE **The forest industry often claims clearcutting benefits wildlife by increasing open forage, but clearcuts soon fill with dense second growth that chokes off sunlight, creating a kind of biological desert in the inner forest.**

almost total uncertainty with respect to the sustainability of future forests."All we propose is to save a working sample of the original while this last opportunity remains.

STICKING TO THEIR STORY THAT IT IS JUST NATURE'S way to liquidate an entire 10,000-year-old rainforest in a little over one human lifetime, industry spokespeople often claim wildlife can cope just fine with the massive disturbance created by industrial logging. Responding to the Great Bear proposal, a Western Forest Products spokesman was quoted as saying logging can coexist with grizzly bears, citing as evidence Western's long-term operation in the Kimsquit Valley. But a report on Kimsquit Valley grizzlies completed by the BC Ministry of Environment in 1989 states: "Grizzly bear abundance apparently declines with logging, but it is unclear whether declines are due to habitat change, excessive killing during and after logging, or other factors." Like other wilderness-dependent species, grizzlies do not necessarily disappear immediately, but their numbers are steadily plunging toward extinction and much of their decline is associated with logging.

THE BC GOVERNMENT AND THE FOREST INDUSTRY admit that irresponsible logging practices did cause unnecessary environmental damage in the past, but they claim a new, responsible approach to logging has brought all that to an end. The centrepiece of the new approach is the Forest Practices Code, implemented in 1995 by then premier Mike Harcourt who used it to head off environmentalist-led boycotts of BC wood products in Europe and the US. "We've stopped the chop," Harcourt assured international audiences. "We've changed practices drastically…We are reducing the size of clearcuts and we are banning clearcuts where necessary to protect critical wildlife habitat, fish bearing streams and other sensitive forest values." So successful was the government's campaign that 72 percent of BC residents polled in 1996 believed clearcutting had either ended, was used just half the time, or was being phased out. However, an audit by the Sierra Legal Defence Fund of 10,000 cutblock approvals issued under the Forest Practices Code found that clearcutting was the designated silvicultural

system in 97 percent of those located on the coast. Far from stopping the chop, timber production in BC actually increased by 2 percent under the first full year of the Code. Across the province, the government permitted loggers to remove slightly over 70 million cubic metres of timber even though the Ministry of Forests itself estimated the long-term sustainable level could be as low as 50 million cubic metres. In the North Coast and Mid-Coast Timber Supply Areas where the Great Bear Rainforest is located, the government permitted loggers to remove 1.6 million cubic metres of timber in 1996, despite a ministry estimate that the long-term sustainable cut for the area was only 851,000 cubic metres. In other words, the Great Bear Rainforest was being logged at double the sustainable rate.

Hopes that wildlife would be safeguarded in this brave new era soon evaporated. When the BC Ministry of Environment, Lands and Parks commissioned a study to find out how well loggers were following fisheries guidelines on the north coast in 1993, Tripp Biological Consultants reported at least one major or moderate impact on every fish-rearing stream examined. Further studies by the Sierra Legal Defence Fund after implementation of the Forest Practices Code found no apparent improvement. Operators logging around known fish streams were allowed to clearcut to the water's edge 79 percent of the time, and operators were allowed to drag logs through streams in 36 percent of cases, both highly destructive practices. In 1996 the provincial government acted on pressure from the loggers' union to oppose endangered species legislation by the federal government, and in June 1997 they rewrote the Forest Practices Code, seriously weakening its environmental impact. None of these developments do much to allay fears the fragile watersheds of the raincoast will suffer devastating damage from BC-style clearcut logging.

WHEN THE CAMPAIGN TO SAVE THE GREAT BEAR RAINFOREST began in earnest in early 1997, forest industry spokesmen reacted as though it posed a mortal threat to the BC economy, warning of potential job losses in the many thousands. Premier Glen Clark pronounced the campaigners "enemies of British Columbia" and the town council of Port Hardy, a logging centre on northern Vancouver Island, passed a

OPPOSITE **This clearcut along the Sleeman and Pike valleys adjacent to Devastation Channel was completed under provisions of the BC Forest Practices Code, offering another example of what the BC government means by world class logging standards.**

resolution denying campaigners access to municipal services. But the economic impact of saving the Great Bear Rainforest would be far smaller than such strong reactions suggest.

Contrary to reports, the Great Bear Proposal would not bring a halt to logging on the northern coast. In valleys where it is already under way, which includes many of the larger and more productive timber growing sites, logging would be free to carry on, and if it were put on a sustainable basis, could continue producing jobs indefinitely. The roughly estimated 224,000 hectares of productive forest actually within the proposal area has a potential to produce future logging jobs, but these would be in the hundreds, not the thousands. If saved to become the world's most outstanding ancient temperate rainforest reserve, the area could have considerable job creation potential in such fields as research and ecotourism, not to mention a healthy salmon fishing industry.

In general, job losses caused by environmental protection in BC have been minor compared to losses from other causes, like government measures to reduce overcutting and industry automation, which eliminated over 20,000 jobs in the 1980s. Most observers agree the best way to reverse job loss in the BC forest industry would be to increase production of higher-quality products for which rainforest wood is better suited, like furniture and fine paper, but the industry prefers to churn out bulk commodities like raw pulp and two-by-four studs because this makes a quicker return on investment. The conservation movement merely serves as a convenient scapegoat for the job-killing effects of this industrial strategy.

The arguments go on and on without resolution while the last of the temperate rainforest disappears. On the raincoast, the old pattern of cut and run continues with little benefit to indigenous people. Most of the loggers are flown in from the south, and the timber is barged away for processing. Typical operations like Western Forest Products' logging camps on Roderick and Yeo islands are temporary affairs using Atco trailers and floating bunkhouses that can be moved from one valley to the next, leaving nothing but stumps and tree plantations. As former treeplanters we have seen this sight time and again. All the government really achieves by pushing logging companies to clearcut the Great Bear Rainforest at double-quick time is to hasten the day when First Nations and others who live there will have no logging jobs, no fishing jobs, no canned salmon to age on the shelf and no cathedral groves of giant spruce left to protect species that we are just beginning to learn about.

THE POINT IS NOT TO CONDEMN particular politicians or companies, but to show why it is necessary to remove something as priceless as the last great rainforest from political and economic processes which by their nature cannot deal with the kind of long-term values involved. The values that abide in the river valleys of the raincoast cannot be measured in dollars and cents. They must be measured in clean water, in strong runs of wild salmon, in healthy wildlife populations, and in a healthy forest environment. Even in crass economic terms, a logging job that might last five years makes little sense when compared to the long-term benefits of saving one of the earth's rarest natural resources—temperate rainforest wilderness. The forest companies are required to submit five-year plans for their proposed logging activities—a five-year development plan for a 10,000-year-old rainforest. The Great Bear Rainforest proposal offers coastal communities a chance to develop a thousand-year plan for the coast, one that will stand the test of time and continue to offer opportunity, food and life for future generations. ■

ABOVE **Using mass-volume technology like this self-dumping log barge, the BC government is allowing the Great Bear Rainforest to be logged at a rate its own Ministry of Forests admits is double the long-term sustainable level.**

OPPOSITE **Falls in the Kiltuish valley. The Great Bear Rainforest is a magnificent and irreplaceable work of nature, and it is in our power to save it.**

ACKNOWLEDGEMENTS

A book of this size on a coast so large could only be built with the help of countless people. We would like to give our heartfelt thanks to Frances Hunter for her commitment to the Raincoast and for her touch of magic in the design of this book, and to Cameron Young for initiating this book project—and for speaking for the rainforest.

We want to express our deep appreciation to Peter McAllister for having had the foresight to organize that first Koeye trip and for being the driving force behind the Raincoast Conservation Society.

Thanks are due as well to Baden Cross and Cindy Lee for the Raincoast voyage aboard the *Sinbad*, and to Sven Johannson for help in past Raincoast Expeditions aboard the *North Star of Herschel Island* and to Erin and Brian Falconer of the *Maple Leaf*.

In addition we wish to thank the following people for their support over the years: Tamara Stark, Karen Mahon and Tzeporah Berman with special thanks to Paul George, Adriane Carr, Chris Genovali and Misty MacDuffee, Simon Waters, Gavin Edwards and Greg Higgs, Vicky Husband and Merran Smith, Jill Thomas, Dennis Sizemore, Bruce Baizel and Jerry Scoville, Wayne McCrory, David Boyd and Greg McDade, Adrian Dorst, Doug Cowell, Bristol Foster, Gary Gagné, Woody and Edie Gagné, Barrie Gilbert, Robert Hall, Tony Hamilton, Stephan Himmer, Marge Housty and Larry Jorgenson and family, Max Johnson, Rolf Hussinger, Bryan McGill at *Beautiful BC*, Ruth Masters, Wendy Neilson, Cecil Paul, Kevin Pegg, Doug Peacock, James Powell, Tom Reimchen, Sammy Robinson, Bernadette Mertens, Malcolm Curtis, Ray Smith, Ray Travers, Mary Vickers, Pauline Waterfall, Erica Wheeler, Elroy White, Dean Wyatt, Shari Bondi, Robert Flemming, Frank Hanuse Sr.

Bear Watch, B.C. Wild, and S. G. Power, for financial assistance and equipment donations.

Trevor Pearce of Inland Air, John Waterfall in Waglisla, Wilderness Air in Bella Coola, Cooper Air, Mid Coast Air, and a special thanks to Les Welsh and the competent pilots of Lighthawk.

The creekwalkers of the coast — Chad and Leanne White on *Kum-Bah-Yah*; Stan Hutchings and Karen Hansen on *Bluefin*; Doug and Carol Stewart on the *Surfbird*; John Lewis on the *Frances M.*; Dave Lewis on the *Princeton*; and Lee Harvey on the *Salty Dog*.

Lens and Shutter in Victoria, especially Simon Desrochers; Custom Color for superb film processing; Broad Street Cameras and Doug who valiantly "kept the wildlife out of Ian's cameras," and Michael Foort for the loan of camera equipment.

Tim McAllister and Tamela Hart, who accompanied us on the trips into the high country; Rami Rothkop for our Quaal River and other adventures; Peter, Glenna and Mark Schulz for the Skowquiltz and Knight Inlet journeys, and Blair LeGallais and Michelle Earl for the shared days sailing on the Raincoast.

We are grateful for the mapping assistance we received from Baden Cross and Tim Wilson.

We would also like to thank Harbour Publishing, especially Howard White and Mary Schendlinger, and Roger Handling of Terra Firma Digital Arts.

A special thanks to Jane McAllister who has given us her ceaseless encouragement and support throughout this project and kept more than one BC Tel radio operator in stifled mirth declaring over the radio phone, "Have you been eaten by any bears yet?"

We also wish to acknowledge the memory of Michael Humphries, who selflessly gave us access to the air, and we are especially beholden to Amelia for being "top ground crew."

As well, we acknowledge the memories of Eve Howden and Randy Stoltmann, and the legacy Humphries, Howden and Stoltmann have left behind.

Ian and Karen McAllister

I wish to express my deepest thanks to Anne, who keeps reminding me where the wildflowers grow, and to Jenny, who fills our lives with music. And I wish to acknowledge the memory of friend and colleague Charles Lillard, who loved the coast

Cameron Young

For more information on the Great Bear Rainforest campaign or to find out how you can help, contact the Raincoast Conservation Society, P.O. Box 26, Bella Bella, BC, V0T 1B0 Canada.

POSTSCRIPT

We write this postscript almost ten years to the day that this book was first published, and many things have happened in the Great Bear Rainforest during this time.

On Feb 7, 2006, the provincial Liberal Government announced conservancy designations for approximately 1.6 million hectares or 30% of the Great Bear while further committing to an "Ecosystem Based Management" (EBM) approach for the remainder of the coast by March 31st, 2009. The agreement was backed up by a $120 million fund earmarked for first nation communities, half raised by environmental groups and the other half matched by the provincial and federal governments.

First nation leaders, elected officials, environmentalists and timber executives stood together at the signing ceremony in Vancouver and protection of the Great Bear was reported in media outlets from South Africa to Moscow, with many of the headlines describing the agreement as a "victory for the rainforest." At first glance, it seemed that the Great Bear had finally and deservedly found its place among the planet's special places that would be protected for generations to come.

However, the Premier of British Columbia, Gordon Campbell, acknowledged on that day that much work remained to be done to save the Great Bear Rainforest. In particular, the level of protection falls short of the recommendations put forward by leading independent scientists hired by the provincial government to provide a land use plan for the Great Bear.

The scientists reported that a low risk option would have 70% of the coastal old growth forests left standing. The agreement announced in 2006 protected approximately 30%, but its proponents argue that if the rest of the Great Bear is managed according to an ecosystem-based management (EBM) approach, the forest and its creatures would still survive. In other words, if human activities outside of the protected areas were carried out in a manner consistent with the EBM approach including the scientists' recommendations, the Great Bear would not need such a high level of core protection.

In theory, this conservation approach sounds reasonable, but the large scale clearcutting that took place shortly after the agreement was announced, coupled with the uncertainty of government living up to its agreements on EBM, especially over the long term, leaves us deeply concerned. We don't believe that the Great Bear, supporting one of the rarest forest types on the planet, should be used as a testing ground for a management policy that has unproven conservation merit in addition to dubious and questionable government support.

Second, the areas that have received conservancy designation could still be threatened by road development, massive tourism operations and the hunting of carnivores such as wolves and grizzly bear. First Nations, Government and environmentalists have yet to develop management plans that truly protect these areas. Further complicating the integrity of the Great Bear agreement are the ongoing and emerging industrial threats to the coast.

Salmon, the undisputed coastal keystone species is increasingly threatened by the provincial government's plan to expand salmon farms in the Great Bear's pristine waters.

For 35 years a government-supported moratorium on tanker traffic and offshore oil and gas exploration on the BC north coast ensured no oil spills or Exxon Valdez-type disasters would occur. Now both the federal and provincial governments are working to lift the moratorium to open the Great Bear up to oil interests. If they succeed, it will not be a matter of if a catastrophic spill happens, but when.

Shortly after conservancy designations were finalized, wind farm companies began proposing massive turbine farms within their boundaries. The wind farm proposed, as an example, within the new conservancy on Banks Island could involve a transmission line to Kitimat 35 meters wide and 150 kilometres long—the largest permanent clearcut ever proposed for the Great Bear.

On the positive side, sustainable, community-based economic development projects are also emerging as a new conservation based economy becomes the new business model.

The Great Bear remains one of the richest ecological and cultural treasures left on the planet. With its comparatively low human population, we believe it is still possible to protect the remaining intact rainforest river valleys and offshore islands while building an economy that provides truly sustainable employment for generations to come.

The countless voices from around the world that have spoken up in support of protecting the Great Bear Rainforest have made a significant and measurable difference, please consider adding yours to this remarkable coastal legacy.

Karen and Ian McAllister